An Invitation to Computer Science

Laboratory Manual

C++ Edition

Kenneth Lambert

Thomas Whaley

Department of Computer Science

Washington and Lee University

THOMSON

COURSE TECHNOLOGY

Australia • Canada • Mexico • Singapore • Spain • United Kingdom • United States

An Invitation to Computer Science Laboratory Manual: C++ Edition is published by Course Technology

Disclaimer
Course Technology reserves the right to revise this publication and make changes from time to time in its content without notice.

ISBN 0-534-39099-4

Contents

Preface

This manual and the downloadable software are intended to give students hands-on experience with the fundamental concepts of computer science. Each lab experience assumes that the student has read a chapter in the textbook that introduces and discusses the concepts presented. For example, Lab Experiences 4 and 6 on sorting algorithms assume that the student has read Chapter 3 of the textbook.

In cases where there is more than one lab section that covers concepts presented in a chapter of the textbook, the first section should be considered an introduction to the material, while the second section provides more advanced exposure. For example, there are introductory and advanced labs on C++ programming, logic circuits, and Turing machines.

Each lab experience begins with a brief discussion of the objectives of the lab experience. Then the student is introduced to the software module that will be used to explore the concepts. Finally, exercises are provided in each lab experience.

The lab manual and software are designed for flexible use:

1. Ideally, students work during a formal lab period with instructor and/or lab assistants available. However, students may also work on their own if no formal lab period is scheduled. Students may work individually or together.

2. Students may do all of the exercises provided in the manual, or the instructor or lab assistant may choose which exercises to require of students, or may add or modify exercises as needed.

3. Most lab work may be turned in either as hard copy or electronically as files.

4. Students may use data files provided with the software, but instructors or lab assistants may add to these files or modify them with the software as needed.

Please note that the software is for your use only; copying it for the purpose of resale or giving it to others is a violation of federal law (as discussed in Chapter 15 of the text).

Please also note that the lab manual comes with tear-out sheets for providing answers to exercises; reproduction of these sheets without the permission of the publisher is also a violation of law.

Changes to the Revised Edition

The visual appearance of the lab software has been made more attractive. Its functionality is similar to that of earlier editions, but three new labs—on networks, discrete event simulation, and data encryption—have been added. The software was written in Java and will run on Windows, UNIX, and Macintosh platforms (see installation instructions below). A new lab on database management has also been added.

Installation Instructions

To download the lab software, go to the Course Technology Web site at

www.course.com/invitation

There you will see further instructions for downloading the version of the lab software for your particular platform.

Windows and UNIX users will also have to download the Java Runtime Environment (JRE), version 1.4 or higher, from Sun at http://java.sun.com/.

Windows and UNIX users should run the installation program for the JRE or JDK to install Java on their machines. After installing the lab software, these users can double-click on the file **Invitation.jar** or enter the command **java -jar Invitation.jar** at the command prompt to launch the lab software. UNIX users may want to change the look and feel to Motif, and Windows users may want to change the look and feel to Windows. To do this, press the **Set Look and Feel** button in the main window. The default look and feel is Metal and is shown in this manual.

Macintosh users should be running OS X 1.2 or higher. They need to download the file **Invitation.jar** and launch it from the **Finder**.

Acknowledgments

We are grateful to the many reviewers of the lab software for their helpful comments. The authors also appreciate the extensive feedback from users of the previous editions of the lab manual and software. If you would like to comment on this new edition, or have found an error in the lab manual or software, please send your information to klambert@wlu.edu.

Lab Experience 1

A Glossary and Web Browsing

Welcome to the laboratory. This manual and the accompanying software will provide you with tools to master and enjoy the fundamental concepts of computer science. You should find these tools easy to use. We assume only that you are familiar with the use of a keyboard and a mouse; if you are not, please consult your lab assistant or instructor. Most of the chapters will begin with a set of objectives for the laboratory session. Then there will be a background section giving any information not covered in the text but which is needed for the exercises. Information will also be given on how to use the software module for the particular topic. Finally, there will be a set of exercises.

Objectives

- Become familiar with the general structure of the lab software
- Practice rudimentary skills that are used in most of the labs
- Learn to use an application that allows you to maintain a glossary of terms
- Begin exploring the World Wide Web (in case you have never done that)

Background

The software consists of an application file and a folder containing some example programs. You should run the software by double-clicking on the application icon. After closing the sign-on dialog box, you should see the menu of buttons as shown in Figure 1.1.

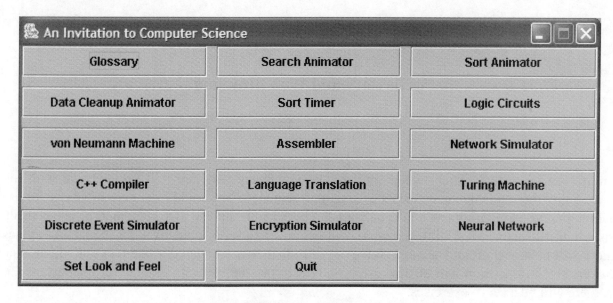

Figure 1.1 The lab software modules

Most of the labs in the course use at least one of the software modules whose names appear in the buttons. These buttons resemble push buttons on real devices such as pocket calculators. You run the function named by the button by clicking once with the mouse on the button. Thus, you open up a software module for the computer science lab with a single click on a button. At this point, UNIX users might want to set the look and feel to Motif and Windows users might want to set the look and feel to Windows. To do this, click the **Set Look and Feel** button and select the desired look and feel. Or you can keep the Metal look and feel, which is shown in this manual. Now click on the **Glossary** button to open the first lab module.

Window basics

Each lab module opens a window that displays information. The glossary window appears as in Figure 1.2. The window has a title—in this case, **Glossary**—at the top. This window presents you with a view of the different components of a virtual glossary. A printed glossary normally appears at the end of a textbook. It lists important terms and their definitions in alphabetical order. Occasionally, a textbook will have a glossary of important terms at the end of each chapter. An electronic glossary makes browsing for the definitions of terms much easier. Note that our glossary window is divided into smaller parts or panes. Each pane has a label describing the kind of information that appears in it. Right now, the window is opened on an empty glossary, but you can see that there are separate panes for displaying chapter titles, terms within a chapter, and the definition of a term. Our glossary window provides you with a simple tool for creating and maintaining glossaries and for displaying and finding the information in them.

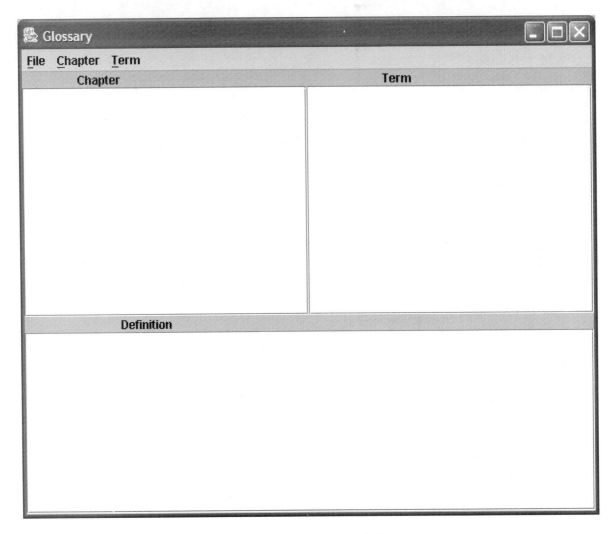

Figure 1.2 The glossary window

Menu basics

At the top of the window, you will see a menu bar. Along the menu bar are a series of one or more names, like **File**, that refer to pull-down menus. You pull down a menu by holding the mouse button down on the menu's name in the menu bar. Try that for **File** now. The commands under **File** usually are **New, Open, Save, Save as,** and **Quit**.

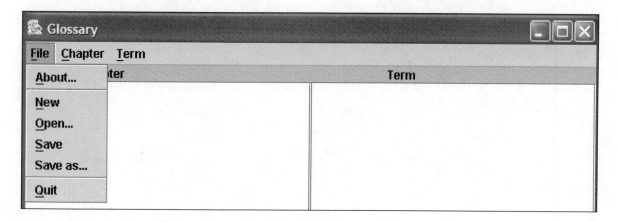

Figure 1.3 The glossary menu bar with File menu selected

You select a command from a pull-down menu by dragging the mouse to the desired command and releasing the mouse button. **New** creates a new, empty glossary. It will also have the effect of erasing any information from a glossary that happens to be displayed in the window. **Open** allows you to open a file containing a glossary and display it in the window. **Save** allows you to save the glossary displayed in the window to a file. **Save as** allows you to save the glossary to a different file. **Quit** appears in every **File** menu and allows you to exit the application.

Opening files

Your software comes with a file that contains a glossary for the first two chapters of the textbook. Select **Open** from the **File** menu. You will be presented with a dialog box that allows you to browse for and select a file to open. The initial dialog box for each lab software module connects to a folder named **Examples** and shows just those files that can be opened for the module (see Figure 1.4).

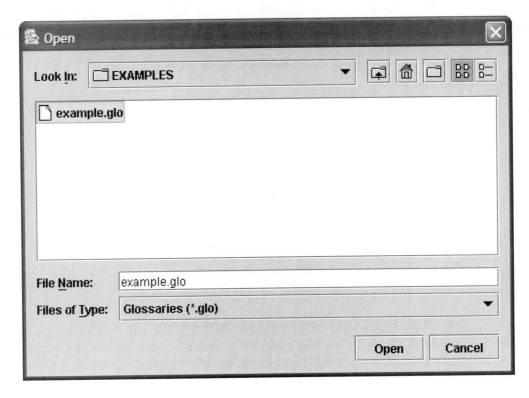

Figure 1.4 A dialog box with a glossary file selected

The names of files containing glossaries, if there are any, will appear in a list. Your options at this point are to open a selected file, select a different file to open, move to a different folder or disk drive to browse for files, or cancel the operation altogether. For now, open the sample file called **example.glo** by selecting it and clicking the **Open** button or pressing the **Enter** key. If all goes well, you should see the contents of the sample glossary in the glossary window.

Browsing for information

You view the terms defined for the first chapter by clicking on its title. You should see a list of terms in the **Term** pane. You can switch to the terms for another chapter by selecting that chapter with the mouse. Try that for the second chapter now, and watch the changes in the **Term** pane. To view the definition of a given term, select any term in the **Term** pane. You should see the definition in the **Definition** pane. Once again, you can switch to the definition of any other term by selecting the term in the **Term** pane. You can also make more terms visible by scrolling through the **Term** pane.

An electronic glossary makes browsing easy and natural. Rather than turning pages of a book to find the end of the desired chapter, and then turning more pages to find the desired term, you click the mouse a couple of times to find a definition of a term in a chapter. In fact, our glossary is just a particular application of a simple electronic database that could serve just as well to organize information according to some other hierarchical scheme of classification.

Searching for information by query

Another way to find the definition of a term is to click the option **Find** that appears in the **Term** menu. You will be prompted for the name of the term whose definition you desire to look up, as shown in Figure 1.5.

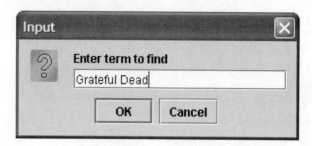

Figure 1.5 Running a query for a term

You type the term at the keyboard, and click **OK** or press **Enter** to start the search. Alternatively, you can click **Cancel** to back out of a query. If the system cannot find the term anywhere in the glossary, it will inform you with a message dialog box, as shown in Figure 1.6.

Figure 1.6 A failed query

When you click **OK** in the message dialog box, you will be allowed to continue working with the glossary. If the term is found, however, the panes in the window will be refreshed so that the chapter and target term are selected and the definition of the term is displayed. Try a query for a term that you know is in the glossary now.

Editing a glossary

The glossary application allows you to edit an existing glossary or build one up from scratch. The application behaves like a word processor with respect to files. The information that you edit in the window is just a working copy of the permanent glossary in a file. If you want to make your changes permanent, you should pick **Save** from the **File** menu. If you want to back out of the changes you have made, you can pick **Open** from the **File** menu to recover an existing glossary or **New** from the **File** menu to start over.

Let's start a new glossary. Select **New** from the **File** menu to clear the window. Then pull down the **Chapter** menu. As shown in Figure 1.7, you will see two choices, of which only **Add** is active.

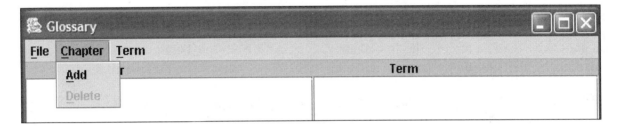

Figure 1.7 Adding a chapter to the glossary

When you select **Add**, the system prompts you for the title of a chapter to be added to the glossary, as shown in Figure 1.8.

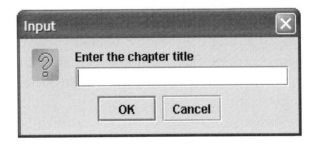

Figure 1.8 Entering the title of a chapter

If you click **OK**, the window will display the chapter title (such as Chapter 1) you entered in the **Chapter** pane. Now pull down the **Term** menu. Note that only **Add** seems to be active in this menu. **Delete** is not active because no term has been selected for deletion. See Figure 1.9.

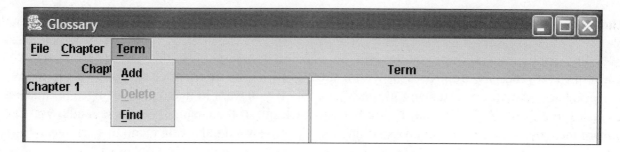

Figure 1.9 Adding a term to the glossary

This is an example of a user-friendly interface: the system provides cues on the screen that tell you what you're allowed to do with the data that is available.

Now you are ready to add a term to the first chapter. Pick **Add** from the **Term** menu. You will be prompted for a new term. Type in **computer science**, and click **OK**. Your window should look like Figure 1.10.

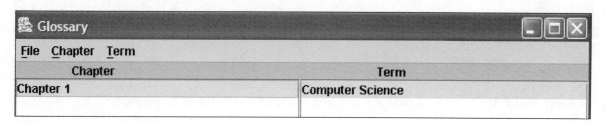

Figure 1.10 The glossary after adding a term

To enter the definition of this term, start typing in the definition. If you don't remember the definition, you can type in a reasonable definition since this part is just for practice anyway. As you type, you will see your words in the **Definition** pane. When you have finished entering the definition, it would probably be a good idea to save your glossary in a file. Select **Save** from the **File** menu and enter a new name (like **myglossary.glo**).

Editing text within text panes

After you have entered the definitions of terms in a glossary, you can return to edit them whenever you like. The pane of the window in which a definition appears is called a text pane. The standard shortcut keys for editing commands are associated with any text pane. For example, on a Windows platform, these commands are Ctrl-X, Ctrl-C, and Ctrl-V for **Cut**, **Copy**, and **Paste**, respectively. These commands assume that you have selected an area of text and wish to manipulate the area with the command. You select text in a text pane by clicking the mouse at the beginning of the area, and holding the mouse button down while dragging the mouse to the end of the area. It may take a couple of tries to get the technique of selection right. When you succeed, the desired chunk should appear in inverse video (white letters on a black background).

Deletion is the simplest (and most dangerous) command. It deletes the text from the pane, and you will not be able to recover the deleted text (except by reopening a permanent file). An easy way to delete a selected area of text is to hit the **Delete** or **Backspace** key on the keyboard. The other three commands utilize a temporary area of computer memory called a *buffer* for saving the selected chunk of text, so that you can restore it to the pane if you wish. **Cut** removes the selected chunk from the pane, and saves it in the buffer. **Copy** saves the selected area in the buffer, but does not remove it from the pane. When you wish the selected area in the buffer to be restored to the pane, you click the mouse at the desired position in the pane and press the shortcut key for **Paste**. Go ahead and try all of these commands now on some sample text.

Introductory Web navigation

In Chapter 7 of the text you will learn a great deal about networks, the Internet, and the World Wide Web. For our purposes now, we can view the "Web" as a large number of **hypertext** documents, called **pages**, which are stored on computers around the world and are generally accessible to the public. A page may contain text, graphics, video, and sound, as well as **links** to other locations within the page or to other pages on the Web. A link is a highlighted item of text or an icon that can be clicked to move to another Web location. Each page has its own address, called a **Uniform Resource Locator** or **URL.** Associated with a link is the URL of the target location.

Among the many types of software available for working with the Web are **Web browsers** that enable you to navigate the Web by specifying URLs and following links, **search engines** that search the Web for specified topics, and **Web editors** for creating and editing Web pages. In order to access the Web, you will need to make use of one of the Web browsers. Two popular browsers at the time of writing of this manual are Netscape Navigator and Microsoft Internet Explorer. Either of these has the basic features that you will need for doing the Web exercises of this manual. Figure 1.11 shows the main menu bar for Internet Explorer. Modern Web browsers have many capabilities other than simply navigating the Web. These include managing e-mail, downloading documents and software from other computers to your computer, and participating in user groups with people of common interests. Here we shall focus on the most basic operations of Web navigation. If you have not used a Web browser, you will need to become familiar with the browser on the system you are using. As you work with the browser more, you will learn more of the advanced features from classmates, lab assistants, the extensive online help systems included with the browsers, and by just trying new things on your own.

Figure 1.11 A Web browser

A user of a browser can set a specific Web page to be his or her **home page**. This is the page that is accessed when the browser is first started. The home page may be a page that the individual has created with his or her personal information, or it may be the main page of the school or company that owns the computer system being used. This page serves as a "home base" for the user. You can always return to your home page by clicking on the **Home** button (labeled with an icon). Once you have a Web page on your screen, you can read the page just like any other computer document; i.e., you read the page on the screen and use scroll devices as needed. However, if you encounter a highlighted object on the page, chances are that this is a link to another page. You can tell whether or not the item is a link by moving the cursor over the item. If it is a link, the cursor will change to a particular shape, say a hand with pointing finger, to indicate a link at the spot. If you click on the link, the browser will attempt to locate the page using the associated URL. This may simply move to another location on the same computer or possibly to a page on a computer half way around the world. If the browser is successful, the target page will appear on your screen. The time it takes to obtain the page depends on several factors such as the traffic on the network at the time, the network distance of the target machine, the speed of the network connections used for the retrieval, and the size of the page. You will find that pages with lots of images take much longer to access. You will have a good understanding of why this is true once you have studied Chapter 7 of the text. Unsuccessful attempts by the browser to locate a page may be due to the fact that the computer with the target page is not available at the time, the URL for the page has been changed, or the author of the page has removed the page. As you navigate through the Web, the browser keeps a history of the URLs that you have visited. At times you may want to reverse your steps for a few pages. You do this by clicking on the **Back** button. Each time you click the Back button, you move to the immediately preceding page in your journey. If you wish to move to a page that you accessed many steps earlier, pull down the **Go** menu. There you will find a list of many of pages that you have accessed. If you know the URL of a page you would like to visit, you simply type the URL into the **Address** field and hit **Enter** on the keyboard. You will learn more about URLs in Chapter 9 of the text. For now, just type the URLs exactly as given. Another feature provided by the browsers is the ability to maintain a list of **bookmarks**. If you find a page that you know you will want to visit on future occasions, you don't have to remember the URL yourself; instead, you can pull down the **Favorites** menu and select **Add to Favorites** (Internet Explorer) or **Bookmarks** (Netscape Navigator). The browser will then add the URL of the current page to its list of bookmark URLs. If you ever wish to go to such a page, you simply pull down the Bookmark menu and select the page you would like to access.

Exercise 1.1. Adding terms to a glossary

Open the glossary that came with the lab software. Click on "Chapter 1: An Introduction to Computer Science" in the Chapter pane. This should bring up the list of terms for Chapter 1 of the text. One term that is missing from Chapter 1 is "unambiguous operation". Choose **Add** from the **Term** menu and enter this term. Type in the definition for this term:

An operation that can be understood and carried out directly
without needing to be further simplified or explained.
(Section 1.3.1)

Now select "Chapter 2: Algorithm Discovery and Design" and add the term "infinite loop" with the
following definition:

A loop in which the termination condition is never met, thus
resulting in the loop body being executed forever or until
the algorithm is aborted by external intervention. (Section 2.2.3)

Choose **Save** from the **File** menu to make sure your additions are stored permanently.

Exercise 1.2. Adding a new chapter

Choose **Add** from the **Chapter** menu and add "Chapter 3: The Efficiency of Algorithms". Now add the
following two terms for Chapter 3:

efficiency - An algorithm's careful use of resources such as space
and time. (Section 3.2)

benchmarking - Comparative timings used to rate one machine
against another with respect to one specific algorithm, or
for rating how sensitive a particular algorithm is with
respect to variations in input on one particular machine.
(Section 3.2).

Now choose **Save** from the **File** menu to make sure your additions are stored permanently.

Exercise 1.3. Making changes to a definition

Select **Chapter 1** from the **Chapter** pane. Then select the term "algorithm" from the **Term** pane. Here you
should find four definitions: a dictionary definition, an informal definition, a formal definition, and a bad
pun definition. The first three of these are from the text, but the fourth has no place in our glossary. Use the
technique discussed earlier to select the text for this fourth definition. Once you have the text selected, hit
the **Delete** key on your keyboard. Again, be sure to save your changes as before.

Exercise 1.4. Using the Find button

Select **Find** from the **Term** menu and search for the term "pseudocode". The term should be found and
selected from the terms of Chapter 2. Copy the definition into the appropriate place in the Worksheet page

for this lab. Now search for the term "unambiguous operation". If things go well, the definition you added earlier should be retrieved. Finally, try finding the term "assembly language". As you see, this term is not covered in the chapters we have in the glossary so far.

Exercise 1.5. Turning in your work

If you have network access, turn in your glossary file from the previous exercises to your instructor (instructions for doing this will vary from school to school; your instructor will have to show you how to do this). Now, under the **File** menu, select **Quit**. This should return you to the main Lab Software window. There you should click on the **Quit** button.

Exercise 1.6. The Web browser and your home page

Follow your local instructions to start up your Web browser. Click on the **Home** button to be sure you have your home page active. Look in the **Location** field to find the URL of your home page. Copy this URL into the appropriate place on the Worksheet.

Exercise 1.7. Accessing a page by URL

Now you should practice accessing a page by entering a URL. For example, type the URL **www.cs.wlu.edu** into the location field of the browser (refer back to Figure 1.11). When you hit the Enter key, you should see the page of the Computer Science Department at one of America's leading small colleges.

Exercise 1.8. Accessing a page by following a link

Now click **Major Requirements.** This should bring up a page with course requirements for a typical computer science major.

Exercise 1.9. Using the Back button and adding a Bookmark

Now return to the previous page for the Web exercises by clicking on the **Back** button of the browser. Add a bookmark to this page. To do this, choose **Add to Favorites** from the **Favorites** menu (Internet Explorer) or **Add Bookmark** from the **Bookmark** menu (Netscape Navigator).

Exercise 1.10. Home again

Now return to your home page by clicking on the **Home** button of the browser.

Worksheet
Lab Experience 1
A Glossary and Web Browsing

Name: _____

Course: _____

Exercise 1.4. Using the Find button

    Pseudocode:

Exercise 1.6. The Web browser and your home page

    URL of your home page:

Lab Experience 2

Search for a Value

Objectives

- Solidify your understanding of the Search for a Value algorithm (Section 2.3.1 of the text) by working with an algorithm animator
- Use empirical data obtained via the animator to derive a general formula about the performance of this algorithm
- Get a first glimpse at how computer scientists analyze algorithms to obtain measures of performance in terms of the size of the problem to be solved

Background

To begin the lab experience, click the **Search Animator** button on your lab software menu. At this point, a new window will appear (see Figure 2.1). Note the following components:

- An **Algorithm** menu; this menu lets you select the algorithm to run (either search for a given value or search for the maximum value)
- The text of the current algorithm (search for a given value when the window is opened)
- A set of four command buttons (**Run, Step, Reset,** and **Input Data Set**)
- A graphic image of an array of values and a box waiting to be filled with the user's target value
- A slider bar to control the running speed

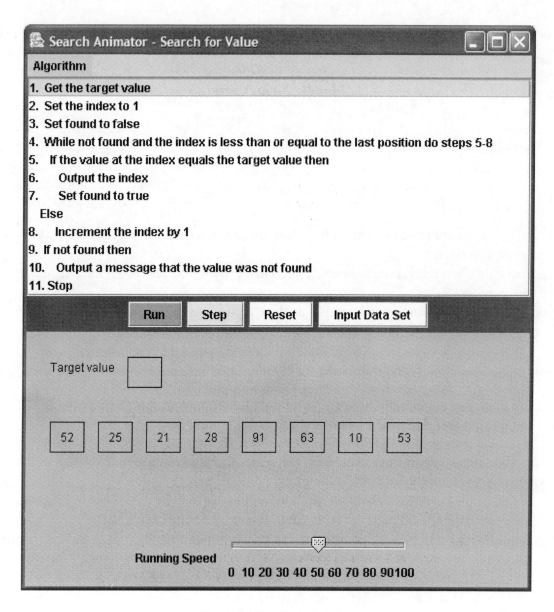

Figure 2.1 The Search Animator

For purposes of this animation, we chose to search through a list of numerical data rather than a list of names. Before each run of the algorithm, you can click on the **Reset** button, and a new set of data will be generated. If for some reason you would like to see how the algorithm performs for some special data set, you can click on the **Input Data Set** button. You will be presented with an array of cells into which you enter the specific values you wish to try. Notice that the first step of the algorithm is shaded. As the execution progresses, the next step to be executed will be shaded. This will enable you to keep track of exactly where the algorithm is in its execution and correlate what is happening to the data on the screen with the step of the algorithm being executed. You will also notice that the pseudocode differs slightly from what is given in the textbook. This was done to correspond with the visual cues given in the animation. Remember that pseudocode is not intended to be rigid and exact, but rather to provide the constructs needed to convey in a fairly precise way how the algorithm performs its task.

When the animator executes the input statement, you will see a prompter box asking you to enter the target value. You should enter the value for which the algorithm should search. Typically, you will enter one of the data values in the list; but if you wish, you may enter a value not in the list to observe what happens in this case. When you enter the target value, you type in the number and then hit the **Enter** key or click on the **OK** button in the prompter box. When an output statement is executed, the output message will appear in a message box. This box will stay on the screen until you hit the **Enter** key or click on the **OK** button.

If you click on the **Run** button, the animator executes the entire algorithm, pausing only for input and output. Clicking on the **Step** button causes just a single step of the algorithm to be executed or pauses execution during a run. Clicking the **Run** button during stepping resumes execution as a run. Given our goals of gaining insight into the nature of the algorithm and gathering empirical data, you will primarily use the step mode of operation.

In the lower-right corner of the animator is a slider bar that adjusts the speed at which the animator runs. By sliding the bar up (faster) or down (slower), you can select a speed that is appropriate for you. It is possible to change from one speed to the another during the animation of the algorithm.

Exercise 2.1. Resetting the data

Click on the **Reset** button a few times and observe what happens to the data set. Explain what seems to be happening on the Worksheet.

Exercise 2.2. Running the animation

Move the slider bar at the bottom of the window to the left to decrease the running speed or to the right to increase it. Click on the **Run** button. Enter as the target value the last value in the data list. As the animation runs, the steps may be executed at a speed that makes the details hard to follow. However, by watching the shaded statement change, you should be able to observe the primary looping nature of the algorithm. Click on the **Reset** button and try this again.

Exercise 2.3. Stepping with the animator

Reset and try out the step mode by clicking on the **Step** button. Enter a value from the middle of the data list and continue stepping by repeatedly using the **Step** button until the stop statement has been executed.

Exercise 2.4. Location of target and number of steps

In this exercise, choose the first element in the list as the target and step through the algorithm. As you step, keep a careful tally of exactly how many times each step is executed. Enter this data into the first row of the table on the Worksheet. Compute the total number of steps executed and enter this into the table. Now reset the animator, use the second data element as the target, and enter the results into the second row of the table. Continue to do this until a distinct pattern becomes apparent. At this point, use the pattern you observe to complete the first eight rows of the table. In the last row of the table, assume that the target is the kth data element and express your entries in terms of k. For example, entries might be k or k+1, etc. Do not fill in the entry in the Total column for the last row.

Exercise 2.5. Formula for the pattern

In this exercise, you will derive a formula that will give the number of steps required by the search algorithm in terms of the position of the target. To do this, simply add the entries in the bottom row of the table from Exercise 2.4 and use algebra to simplify the expression obtained. Give your formula on the Worksheet.

Exercise 2.6. Prediction for larger data set

Based on the pattern observed in Exercise 2.5, how many steps would you expect it to take to find the 100th element, if there were that many in the list? Give your answer on the Worksheet.

Exercise 2.7. Average number of comparisons

As you will see in Chapter 3, one measure of work done by an algorithm is the number of comparisons of elements that the algorithm must perform. In the Search for Value algorithm, the comparisons are made in Step 5. Under the assumption that the target is as likely to be in any one position in the list as in any other position, the best way to measure the number of comparisons is to average the number of comparisons required for the various positions of the target. Compute the average number of times Step 5 must be executed for the eight-element list by averaging the numbers in the first eight rows of the Step 5 column of the table in Exercise 2.4. If the list only had seven elements, we would average the first seven of the numbers in this column. Try computing this average for a few values for the list size. Give a formula for the average number of comparisons if there are n elements in the list.

Worksheet
Lab Experience 2
Search for a Value

Name: _____

Course: _____

Exercise 2.1. Resetting the data

What happens when you click on the Reset button?

Exercise 2.4. Location of target and number of steps

Target Step	Step 1	Step 2	Step 3	Step 4	Step 5	Step 6	Step 7	Step 8	Step 9	Step 10	Total
Element 1											
Element 2											
Element 3											
Element 4											
Element 5											
Element 6											
Element 7											
Element 8											
Element k											

Exercise 2.5. Formula for the pattern

Exercise 2.6. Prediction for larger data set

Exercise 2.7. Average number of comparisons

Average for 8-element list:

Average for 7-element list:

Average for 4-element list:

Average for 2-element list:

Average for n-element list:

Lab Experience 3

Search for the Largest Value

Objectives

- Solidify your understanding of the Search for Largest Value algorithm (Section 2.3.2 of the text) by working with an algorithm animator
- Learn or review some useful combinatorial facts for counting different arrangements of a set
- Use empirical data obtained via the animator together with combinatorics to develop general conjectures about the performance of the algorithm

Background

As in Lab Experience 2, you begin the lab experience by clicking on the **Search Animator** button on your lab software menu. This time, after the search animator window opens, you should select the **Search for Largest** option under the **Algorithm** menu.

In the exercises you will be asked a couple of questions that require the knowledge of two facts from probability. First, if we have n numbers chosen at random (as we get when we click **Reset**), there are

$$n! = n(n-1)(n-2)\cdots(2)(1)$$

different possible orderings of the numbers. For example, with the 8 items in the animator, there would be $8\cdot7\cdot6\cdot5\cdot4\cdot3\cdot2\cdot1 = 40,320$ different orders in which we could list the 8 elements. The idea is that there are n elements from which to choose the first element. Having chosen the first element, there are n-1 elements left from which to choose the second element. Thus there are n(n-1) ways in which to choose the first two numbers in the list. Continuing in this way leads to the formula above.

The second fact has to do with the likelihood that a given item will occur in a given location. The point here is that a given item, in terms of relative size, is as likely to occur in one position as another. So, if there are n items, the probability that a particular one of the items shows up in a specific position would be 1/n. For example, the probability that the second largest item would show up in position 6 when we click **Reset** would be 1/8 with the animator having 8 items. This means that if you reset many, many times, you should see the second largest show up in this position about 1/8 of the time. This would require many trials in order to see this fact play out.

Exercise 3.1. Stepping

Use the **Step** button to execute the algorithm two or three times until you understand exactly how the algorithm works and how the animation corresponds to the steps in the pseudocode window. Remember to click the **Reset** button when you are ready to start over with a new set of data.

Exercise 3.2. How many positions does the location marker achieve?

Observe that with the 8 pieces of data, there are always 7 passes through the loop (n-1 if there were n pieces of data). However, the number of positions that the location marker takes on (Step 7) depends on the relative order of the data. You will now make use of the animator to explore this dependence in more depth. Using the step mode, you should now gather data from 10 executions of the algorithm and enter the results on the Worksheet. For each data set, you should copy down the entire data set and keep up with the position of the location marker L and the data value at position L each time L moves. For example, if the data set were 20,15,25,30,42,18,72,11, then you would copy the entire list as the data set. The original position of L would be position 1, and the value in that position is 20. Therefore, you would enter 1 for the location and 20 for the value. When the L marker moves, list the location that it moves to and the value there. Continue until the algorithm terminates. Once you are sure of how this works, it is fine just to click the **Reset** button and copy the relevant data down without stepping through the entire execution (just be sure that you know what will happen).

Exercise 3.3. Determining the values at the Location marker by scanning

Look at the data obtained in Exercise 3.2. Notice that the values stored in the positions taken on by the Location marker form a *subsequence* of the original data set; i.e., the values of the subset are taken from the original set in the same relative order as in the original set. On the Worksheet, explain in your own words how to scan the list from left to right and pick out the values that will be in this subsequence.

Exercise 3.4. Smallest number of positions for the L marker

What would be the smallest number of positions that Location could possibly take on? Describe the special conditions under which this would happen. Approximately, how often would you expect this to occur? Put your answers on the Worksheet.

Exercise 3.5. Largest number of positions for the Location marker

What would be the largest number of positions that Location could possibly take on? Describe the conditions under which this would happen. Approximately, how often would you expect this to occur? Put your answers on the Worksheet.

Exercise 3.6. Likelihood of many positions for the L marker

How would you compare the likelihood that Location would take on three different values with the likelihood that Location would take on seven different values? Would you expect the likelihood that Location takes on three different values to be much smaller, about the same, or much larger than the likelihood that it would take on seven different values? Answer on the Worksheet.

Worksheet
Lab Experience 3
Search for the Largest Value

Name: _____

Course: _____

Exercise 3.2. How many positions does the location marker achieve?

Data Set 1:   Data Set 6:
Location: Location:
Value: Value:

Data Set 2:   Data Set 7:
Location: Location:
Value: Value:

Data Set 3:   Data Set 8:
Location: Location:
Value: Value:

Data Set 4:   Data Set 9:
Location: Location:
Value: Value:

Data Set 5:   Data Set 10:
Location: Location:
Value: Value:

Exercise 3.3. Determining the values at the Location marker by scanning

Explanation for finding subsequence:

Exercise 3.4. Smallest number of positions for the L marker

Smallest number of positions for Location: _____

Special conditions for this to occur:

How frequently would this occur?

Exercise 3.5. Largest number of positions for the Location marker

Largest number of positions for Location: _____

Special conditions for this to occur:

How frequently would this occur?

Exercise 3.6. Likelihood of many positions for the Location marker

Lab Experience 4

Sort Animations

Objectives

- Use an animator to gain a better understanding of the Selection Sort algorithm (Section 3.3.3 of the text)
- Learn about two other well-known sort algorithms, Bubble Sort (Chapter 3 Exercises) and Quick Sort (covered in the Background Section)
- Study the amount of work done by these algorithms by gathering empirical data on the number of comparisons and/or exchanges they make

Background

One of the most common tasks of computer programs is the sorting of numerical or textual data. This is due to the enormous number of reports that must be produced with the data in a specified order and the enormous number of searches for specified records. As soon as you have compared the efficiency of binary search of ordered data with sequential search of unordered data, you will appreciate the importance of maintaining data in ordered structures in large database systems.

The importance of sorting accounts for the large amount of work that computer scientists have devoted to designing and analyzing various algorithms for sorting data. It may seem that one algorithm would become the "standard" sorting algorithm which everyone would use. This is not the case, however, and most computer programmers have a small collection of such algorithms that they can readily implement or already have implemented. The reason for this is that there are several factors that determine the appropriateness of a specific algorithm. For example, the simple algorithms tend to work well on small sets of data, say 50 or fewer items, but become too slow to be useful on larger sets. Some algorithms work well for data that is somewhat ordered to begin with, while other algorithms do their worst on data already ordered. Some of the least efficient algorithms are popular simply because they are easy to understand and therefore easy to implement by beginning programmers.

The software module for this lab is accessed by clicking on the **Sort Animator** button of the main button menu of the lab software. The various sort algorithms appear as options under the **Sort Algorithm** menu. The selection sort algorithm has been covered thoroughly in the text. Notice that the version here is "expanded," in the sense that the individual steps of the search for largest algorithm of Chapter 2 are included here rather than given as a single step. At the lowest level all of these steps must be carried out. Of course we do not include the steps for obtaining the data since we do not get new data each time the algorithm finds the largest element of the unsorted section. The bubble sort algorithm is a comparable algorithm that is introduced in the exercises at the end of Chapter 3 of the text. The insertion sort algorithm is another "simple" sort algorithm that will not be covered in detail here unless your lab instructor chooses to introduce it. You are certainly encouraged to explore this algorithm on your own. The basic idea is that, moving from the left, each element is "inserted" into its proper sorted position among the elements preceding it in the list.

The selection, bubble, and insertion sort algorithms all have the feature that they make many passes through the data, essentially placing one data item per pass. The effect of this is that these algorithms fall into the same general class in terms of efficiency. To obtain an algorithm that will be fundamentally better requires an entirely different approach. There are sort algorithms that, like the binary search algorithm, are based on the "divide and conquer" strategy for problem solving. For sorting with this strategy, the basic plan is to gain efficiency by sorting pieces of the list and then having some way to put the sorted pieces back together into a sorted whole. The quick sort algorithm is one such algorithm.

The general plan for quick sort is first to partition the elements of the list with the smaller elements going into the first section and the larger elements going into the second section. Once the two sections are themselves sorted, it follows that the entire list will be sorted. The pseudocode for this basic version is:

1. Partition the list with small elements in first part, large elements in second part.
2. Sort the first part.
3. Sort the second part.
4. Stop.

To implement this plan, we must settle two obvious questions: first, how do we accomplish the partitioning of the list, and second, how do the sections get sorted?

Let's deal with the second question first. To sort a sublist, we use the same strategy as on the entire list; i.e., we partition the sublist and sort the remaining sublists. An algorithm like this, which makes use of itself to solve smaller subproblems of the same type, is called a *recursive algorithm*. Binary search is sometimes presented as a recursive algorithm. Clearly, this process of partitioning and applying the sort algorithm to smaller lists must not go on forever. At which point we stop subdividing is somewhat a matter of choice. For our purposes, we will stop if the sublist to be sorted has no more than two elements. If it has only one element, there is nothing more to do, and if it has two elements, we simply compare the elements and exchange them if they are out of order. With this level of refinement, the pseudocode looks like:

1. If the list to sort has more than 1 element then:
2. If the list has exactly two elements then:
3.   If the two elements are out of order then:
4.   Exchange them.
5. Otherwise
6.   Partition list with small elements in first part,
          large elements in second part.
7. Apply Quick Sort to the first part.
8.   Apply Quick Sort to the second part.
9. Stop.

The strategy for the partitioning is to choose an element from the list to serve as a "pivot" element. Then we compare the other elements with the pivot element, putting the elements less than or equal to the pivot into the first section and putting the elements larger than the pivot into the second section. This leads to two more questions—how to choose the pivot and how to get each element into the appropriate section of the list. The ideal pivot element would be the median of the list. This would lead to an even split, which in turn leads to the most efficient sorting. However, it is important that the choice of the pivot element be made quickly; so, it is not feasible to look for the median each time. Some versions of quick sort simply take the first element, others take the median of the first, last, and some middle item, and so on. For the purposes of our animator, we chose to consider the first three elements of the sublist and take the median value of these as the pivot.

Once the pivot element has been chosen, we exchange it with the first element in the sublist. The partitioning algorithm that we use employs two markers, a lower marker (L) that starts at the second element and an upper marker (U) that starts on the last element of the sublist. Now we keep moving L to the right until we come to an element larger than the pivot (everything to the left of L belongs in the first section). Next, we move U to the left until we come to an element smaller than the pivot (elements to the right of U are in the second section). If L and U have not crossed, then the element at L belongs in the second section, and the element at U belongs in the first section; so we exchange them. We continue this process of moving L to the right, moving U to the left, and exchanging until the markers cross. At this point, U should be on the last element of the first section. We then exchange the pivot element with the element at U. The elements to the left of U (the pivot) comprise the first section, and the elements to the right of U comprise the second section. The following is the pseudocode for the version that is used in the animator:

1. If the list to sort has more than 1 element then:
2. If the list has exactly two elements then:
3. If the two elements are out of order then:
4. Exchange them.
5. Otherwise
6. Exchange the median of the first three elements with the first.
7. Set the pivot marker (P) on the first of the elements.
8. Set the lower marker (L) on the second element.
9. Set the upper marker (U) on the last element.
10. While L is not to the right of U do Steps 11-16.
11. While the element at L is not larger than the element at P do Step 12.
12. Move L to the right one position.
13. While the element at U is larger than the element at P do Step 14.
14. Move U to the left one position.
15. If L is left of U then:
16. Exchange the elements at L and U.
17. Exchange the elements at P and U.
18. Apply Quick Sort to the sublist of elements to the left of U.
19. Apply Quick Sort to the sublist of elements to the right of U.
20. Stop.

If you have trouble following this discussion, remember that the purpose of the animator is to help you understand the details of the algorithms. Once you have worked with the animator, matching steps in the pseudocode with the actions in the animation, come back and read these paragraphs again.

Exercise 4.1. Stepping with selection sort

Choose the **Selection Sort** algorithm from the **Sort Algorithm** menu. Click on the **Step** button until you see exactly how the algorithm works. Each time, before clicking, try to anticipate what is going to happen when you click on the button.

Exercise 4.2. Show what would happen with selection sort

Suppose the original data set consists of the numbers

34 52 21 14 67 59 30 18

Show on the Worksheet the exact arrangement of the data after 3 major passes have been made by the selection sort algorithm, where a major pass is completed each time we come back to Step 2.

Exercise 4.3. Counting exchanges and comparisons with selection sort

Click on the **Reset** button and write down on the Worksheet the data set that is generated. Now repeatedly click the **Step** button until the animator completes its task of sorting the data. As you do this, keep track (Worksheet) of how many exchanges are made (Step 9), and also keep track of how many comparisons (Step 6) are made. Do this for each pass, and then get the two totals for the entire sorting.

Exercise 4.4. Compare with the theory for selection sort

How does the total for the number of comparisons obtained in Exercise 4.3 compare with the formula of $(1/2)n^2 - (1/2)n$ given in the text (note that n=8 for the animator)?

How many comparisons would it take for n=20? How many exchanges? Record your answers on the Worksheet.

Exercise 4.5. Stepping with bubble sort

Choose the **Bubble Sort** algorithm from the **Sort Algorithm** menu. Click on the **Step** button until you see exactly how this algorithm works.

Exercise 4.6. Show what would happen with bubble sort

Suppose the original data set consists of the numbers

34 52 21 14 67 59 30 18

Show on the Worksheet the exact arrangement of the data after 3 major passes have been made by the bubble sort algorithm, where a major pass is completed each time we come back to Step 2.

Exercise 4.7. Counting exchanges and comparisons with bubble sort

Click on the **Reset** button and write down on the Worksheet the data set that is generated. Now repeatedly click the **Step** button until the animator completes its task of sorting the data. As you do this, keep track of how many exchanges are made (Step 6), and also keep track of how many comparisons (Step 5) are made. Do this for each pass, and then get the two totals for the entire sorting.

Exercise 4.8. Compare with selection sort

How do the totals for bubble sort (Exercise 4.7) compare with those of selection sort (Exercise 4.3)? How many comparisons would you estimate for bubble sort with n=20? Can we say exactly how many exchanges there will be with n=20? Record your answers on the Worksheet.

Exercise 4.9. Stepping and counting exchanges and comparisons with insertion sort

Choose the **Insertion Sort** algorithm from the **Sort Algorithm** menu. Click on the **Step** button until you see exactly how this algorithm works. Then click on the **Reset** button and write down on the Worksheet the data set that is generated. Now repeatedly click the **Step** button until the animator completes its task of sorting the data. As you do this, keep track of how many exchanges are made (Step 5), and also keep track of how many comparisons (Step 4) are made. Do this for each pass and then get the two totals for the entire sorting. Now reset the animator and enter new numbers into the array *in sorted order* by selecting **Input Data Set**. Record the comparisons and exchanges on the Worksheet as before. Explain any differences in the results for the two data sets.

Exercise 4.10. Stepping with quick sort

Choose the **Quick Sort** algorithm from the **Sort Algorithm** menu. Click on the **Step** button until you see exactly how this algorithm works. Notice that each time the algorithm starts to sort one of its sublists, a begin marker (**lower**) and an end marker (**upper**) mark the beginning and end of the current sublist. Also notice that executing the stop command simply indicates the ending of the work on the current sublist. Be sure you understand the details before moving on.

Exercise 4.11. Show what would happen with quick sort

Suppose the original data set consists of the numbers

34 52 21 14 67 59 30 18

Show on the Worksheet the exact arrangement of the data after the data has been partitioned the first time (when we come to Step 18 the first time).

Exercise 4.12. Counting exchanges and comparisons with quick sort

Click on the **Reset** button and write down on the Worksheet the data set that is generated. Now repeatedly click the **Step** button until the animator completes its task of sorting the data. As you do this, keep track of how many exchanges are made (Steps 4, 6, 16, and 17), and also keep track of how many comparisons of data elements are made (Steps 11 and 13).

Worksheet
Lab Experience 4
Sort Animations

Name: _____

Course: _____

Exercise 4.2. Show what would happen with selection sort

Original data set: 34 52 21 14 67 59 30 18

After 3 passes:

Exercise 4.3. Counting exchanges and comparisons with selection sort

Original data set:

Pass	Exchanges	Comparisons
1		
2		
3		
4		
5		
6		
7		
Totals		

Exercise 4.4. Compare with the theory for selection sort

Compute the value of $(1/2)n^2 - (1/2)n$ with n=8:

How does this compare with the number of comparisons found in Exercise 4.3?

Number of comparisons for n=20:

Number of exchanges for n=20:

Exercise 4.6. Show what would happen with bubble sort

Original data set: 34 52 21 14 67 59 30 18

After 3 passes:

Exercise 4.7. Counting exchanges and comparisons with bubble sort

Original data set:

Pass	Exchanges	Comparisons
1		
2		
3		
4		
5		
6		
7		

Totals

Exercise 4.8. Compare with selection sort

Compare the number of exchanges for bubble sort with selection sort:

Compare the number of comparisons for bubble sort with selection sort:

Number of comparisons with bubble sort for n=20:

Any comments about the number of exchanges with bubble sort:

Exercise 4.9. Counting exchanges and comparisons with insertion sort

Original data set 1:

Original data set 2:

Pass	Exchanges	Set 1	Set 2	Comparisons	Set 1	Set 2
1						
2						
3						
4						
5						
6						
7						

Totals

Explanation of differences:

Exercise 4.11. Show what would happen with quick sort

Original data set: 34 52 21 14 67 59 30 18

After first partitioning:

Exercise 4.12. Counting exchanges and comparisons with quick sort

      Original data set:

      Make tally mark for each exchange:

      Total exchanges:

      Make tally mark for each comparison:

      Total comparisons:

Lab Experience 5

Data Cleanup and Binary Search

Objectives

- Use animators to solidify your understanding of the Shuffle-Left and Converging Pointers algorithms for data cleanup (Section 3.4.1 of the text)
- Use empirical data gathered using the animators to develop a relationship between the number of "copy" operations required and the number and locations of the bad data items in the original data sets
- Explore the binary search algorithm (Section 3.4.2 of the text)

Background

To begin the lab experience, click the **Data Cleanup Animator** button on your lab software menu. Under the **Algorithm** menu, there are options for the **Shuffle-Left** algorithm and the **Converging Pointers** algorithm. Be sure to select the one that applies to the exercise you are currently doing.

For the Shuffle-Left algorithm, the number of times a data item is copied to another position depends not only on the number of bad data items (0's), but also on the positions in which the bad data are located. As you will see, the number of copy operations generated by a given bad data item depends on the position in which the data item is located when it is detected by the if-statement (Step 5 in the animator pseudocode) and on the number of items in the entire list. The position where a bad data item will be detected can be determined by the position of the item in the entire list and by its position in the list of bad data (is it the first bad item, second bad item, etc.). Once these relationships are understood, it is possible to determine the total number of copy operations required, knowing only the original positions of the bad data items. You will explore this connection in the exercises.

For the Converging Pointers algorithm, you will find that the situation is dramatically different as far as the number of copy operations is concerned.

Exercise 5.1. Running the Shuffle-Left animation
Select the **Shuffle-Left** algorithm from the **Algorithms** menu. Use the **Run** button and observe the "loop inside a loop" nature of this algorithm by watching the animation. The general idea is that the L marker moves to the right trying to detect 0's. Each time it detects a 0, the R marker moves to the right shuffling the

data items to the left. Try this three or four times, remembering to use the **Reset** button to prepare for each run.

Exercise 5.2. Stepping with the Shuffle-Left animation

Now use the **Step** button to walk through the algorithm on a couple of data sets. This allows you to see the fine details of how the algorithm works. Once you are comfortable with this, move on to Exercise 5.3.

Exercise 5.3. Copy operations and positions of 0's

Now we will explore the question of the number of copy operations needed to do the data cleanup with this algorithm. This time click the **Reset** button until you get a data set with three or four 0's or use the **Input Data Set** option to enter such a data set. Record the location of the 0's in the original data set on the Worksheet. Now step through the algorithm, carefully observing and recording where each 0 is located when it is detected by the if-statement of Step 5. Also, observe and record how many copy operations (Step 10) are executed as the given 0 is "squeezed out."

Exercise 5.4. Drawing conclusions

In this exercise, you are asked to draw conclusions based upon your observations in Exercise 5.3. It may be that you will need to repeat Exercise 5.3 a time or two before you see the relationships. Record your answers on the Worksheet.

With an 8-element list, if a 0 is detected in position k, how many copy operations are needed to squeeze it out?
Suppose there were n items in the list rather than 8?
If the first 0 is originally in position k, where will it be when it is detected by the if-statement?
If the second 0 is originally in position k, where will it be when it is detected?
If the third 0 is originally in position k, where will it be when it is detected?
If the jth 0 is originally in position k, where will it be when it is detected?
If the first 0 is originally in position k, how many copy operations will it generate?
If the third 0 is originally in position k, how many copy operations will it generate?

Exercise 5.5. Using the conclusions

Using the conclusions you formulated in Exercise 5.4, suppose we have 200 items in the original list with three 0's located in positions 47, 110, and 162. Tell exactly how many copy operations would be performed by the Shuffle-Left algorithm in cleaning up this data set (Worksheet).

Exercise 5.6. Running and stepping with Converging Pointers

Now choose the **Converging Pointers** algorithm from the **Algorithms** menu. As before, you should work with the run and step modes until you have a clear picture of how the algorithm works.

Exercise 5.7. Copy operations with Converging Pointers

Using the step mode, explore the question of the number of copy operations in terms of the number and location of the 0's for this algorithm. For each trial run, write down the data set on scratch paper and keep up with the number of copy operations. Try to find a data set where the number of copy operations is the same as the number of 0's, and record the original data set on the Worksheet. Try to find a data set where the number of copy operations is different from the number of 0's and record this data set. As a **challenge problem**, formulate a clear description of data sets where the number of copy operations is different from the number of 0's. (In other words, how can we tell by looking at the original data set whether the number of copy operations will be the same as the number of 0's?)

Exercise 5.8. Converging Pointers with larger data sets

Answer Exercise 5.5 using the Converging Pointers algorithm instead of the Shuffle-Left algorithm.

Exercise 5.9. Markers and good data items

When the animator completes its run, how can we tell where the good data items are located in terms of the markers?

Exercise 5.10. Binary search

Close the Data Cleanup Lab and open the Sort Animator Lab for this exercise. Click on the **Reset** button to obtain new data in the array. Then pick **Binary Search** from the **Sort** menu. What happens? Why? Now take the appropriate steps to make the array ready to search and step through the binary search algorithm. Notice that each time through the loop, the number at the **mid** marker is compared with the target number. This happens each time **mid** takes on a new value. Therefore, we can count the comparisons by counting the number of positions that **mid** takes on. Using the step mode, first choose the first element in the list as the target and record the number of positions that **mid** takes on. Now repeat this, choosing the second element in the list as the target, and continue for each element in the list. Give the largest number of comparisons made for any target in the list. Give the average number of comparisons. What would be the largest number of comparisons needed to find a target if we had 16 data items rather than 8? How about 32 data items? How about 1024 data items? Record your answers on the Worksheet.

Worksheet
Lab Experience 5
Data Cleanup and Binary Search

Name: _____

Course: _____

Exercise 5.3. Copy operations and positions of 0's

Original position of first 0:
Position where first 0 is detected:
Number of copy operations generated by first 0:

Original position of second 0:
Position where second 0 is detected:
Number of copy operations generated by second 0:

Original position of third 0:
Position where third 0 is detected:
Number of copy operations generated by third 0:

Exercise 5.4. Drawing conclusions

Number of copy operations generated by 0 detected in position k of 8-element list:

Number of copy operations generated by 0 detected in position k of n-element list:

Position where first 0 is detected if it is originally in position k:

Position where second 0 is detected if it is originally in position k:

Position where third 0 is detected if it is originally in position k:

Position where jth 0 is detected if it is originally in position k:

Number of copy operations generated by first 0 in n-element list if it is originally in position k:

Number of copy operations generated by third 0 in n-element list if it is originally in position k:

Exercise 5.5. Using the conclusions

Number of copy operations for 200-element list with 0's in positions 47, 110, and 162:

Exercise 5.7. Copy operations with Converging Pointers

Data set where number of copy operations is same as number of 0's:

Data set where number of copy operations is different from number of 0's:

Challenge - when will number of copy operations differ from number of 0's?

Exercise 5.8. Converging Pointers with larger data sets

Number of copy operations for 200-element list with 0's in positions 47, 110, and 162:

Exercise 5.9. Markers and good data items

Where are the good items in terms of the markers?

Exercise 5.10. Binary search

What happens when you first try to choose Binary Search?

Why should this happen?

Number of comparisons with first number as target:

Number of comparisons with second number as target:

Number of comparisons with third number as target:

Number of comparisons with fourth number as target:

Number of comparisons with fifth number as target:

Number of comparisons with sixth number as target:

Number of comparisons with seventh number as target:

Number of comparisons with eighth number as target:

Largest number of comparisons:

Least number of comparisons:

Average number of comparisons:

Largest number of comparisons if n=16:

Largest number of comparisons if n=1024:

Lab Experience 6

Sort Timing

Objectives

- Learn a new way to view data as it is being sorted
- Interpret the distinctive data patterns generated by different sort algorithms
- Test theoretical results about sort algorithms by using a timer to test predictions based on these results

Background

First, let's discuss how the data being sorted can be viewed graphically as a sort algorithm is executing. The best way to understand this approach is to consider the list of data as a function. Suppose we have the list of numbers 5, 7, 2, 8, 3. Now this list can be viewed as a function, say L, where L(1)=5, L(2)=7, L(3)=2, L(4)=8, and L(5)=3. We can now draw the scatter plot graph of this function as in Figure 6.1. It is interesting and insightful to watch the scatter plot as the list is being sorted. As you will see, the structure of the data at intermediate steps differs significantly depending upon the algorithm being used. Of course these graphs will not show the steps in as much detail as the animator in the previous lab, but they will show the structure of the data in a more useful way. As an example, let's carry through the selection sort algorithm as it works on the data in the list above. The first change that we observe is when the largest element, 8, is exchanged with the last element, 3.

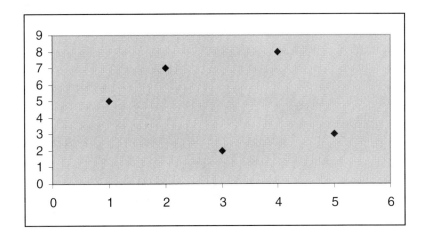

Figure 6.1 Scatter plot graph of a list

After this exchange, we have L(4)=3 and L(5)=8, and the other function values are as before. The resulting scatter plot is shown in Figure 6.2.

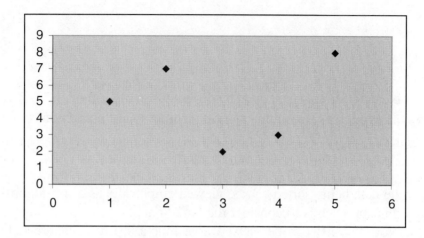

Figure 6.2 Graph after first exchange

The graphs after the subsequent exchanges are shown in Figures 6.3 and 6.4. Even with this tiny data set, you should be able to see clearly the sorted and unsorted sections after each step. The software we use in this lab allows us to watch the scatter plots for several sort algorithms. You will be asked to observe the scatter plots and answer questions relating the patterns formed with the particular algorithm under study.

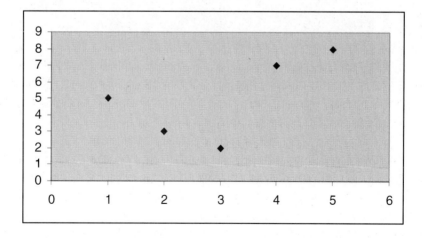

Figure 6.3 Graph after second exchange

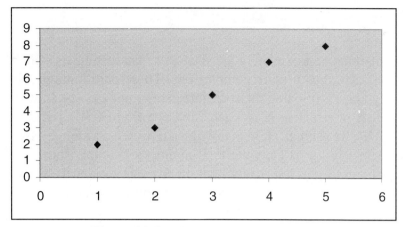

Figure 6.4 Graph after third exchange

The second goal of this laboratory session has to do with timing sort algorithms to see how well the theoretical efficiency classifications hold up in practice. You will be asked to time a given algorithm for a relatively small data set and then, based on the efficiency classification of the sort algorithm, you will make a prediction as to how long that algorithm would take to sort a larger size data set. Then you can do actual runs of the algorithm to see how good your prediction is.

It is important to keep in mind that the classifications are rather crude. For example, we have lopped off all terms except for the dominating term. So, these classifications are useful only to give ball-park estimates or to understand the general growth rate for the algorithm. You should also keep in mind that the performance of most of these algorithms depends on the data to be sorted. We've seen this already when using the sort animator, and by viewing the scatter plots for multiple runs of the same algorithm this will become even more apparent. Also, we should mention that the times being recorded are not fair tests for the algorithms if all that is needed is for the numerical data to be sorted. Here we are timing not only the sorting, but also the graphing of the scatter plots. In general, the graphing is orders of magnitude slower than the internal sorting. As you'll see throughout your study of computer science, manipulations that take place in the memory of the computer are much faster than manipulations with external devices such as printers or monitors.

For the timing exercises, you need to be familiar with the classifications of the algorithms. You recall that selection sort, as analyzed in Section 3.3.3 of the text, is a $\theta(n^2)$ algorithm. A similar analysis of the bubble sort algorithm (see Exercises 8-10 from Chapter 3 of the text and Lab Experience 4) shows that it is also $\theta(n^2)$ as is the insertion sort algorithm.

A complete analysis of the quick sort algorithm is beyond the level of this course, but can be found in most texts on computer algorithms. To get some idea of how this algorithm provides an improvement over the other algorithms considered so far, we'll do a very rough analysis for the idealized situation where we get nearly even splits for all of our partitions. To carry out a partitioning with a list of k elements requires that each element other than the pivot be compared with the pivot, thus k-1 comparisons are required. Depending on how we choose the pivot, another comparison or two may be required. To keep the algebra simple, let's say k comparisons are needed. If we begin with an n element list, then we'll have n comparisons to partition it into two sublists each containing approximately n/2 elements. These sublists will eventually be partitioned, requiring n/2 comparisons each, thus n more comparisons. These partitionings result in four more sublists each of size approximately n/4. Partitioning these requires about n/4 each or another n total. Remember that we stop when we get sublists of size 1 or 2. At each "level" we're requiring about n comparisons. But how many levels will there be? We're asking "How many times must we divide n by two before the result is 1 or 2?" The answer is approximately Lg n. Thus the total number of comparisons in this idealized situation is approximately Lg n times n, or n Lg n. It turns out that the average case analysis also leads to the conclusion that quick sort is a θ(n Lg n) algorithm. One way to think about this is that instead of n^2 , we have one of the n's replaced with Lg n, a fundamental improvement.

As an example of how we might use the Big Oh classifications to make predictions, suppose we run a sort on a list of size 1000 using selection sort, and suppose it takes 1 second to complete the sort. Let's use this information to obtain a rough approximation of how long it would take the same algorithm on the same computer to sort a list of size 100,000. Since selection sort is dominated by an n^2 term, we can use the formula $T(n) \cong K n^2$ where T(n) is the time to sort n elements, K is some constant, and $\cong$ indicates approximation. Now K can be approximated using the given information:

$$T(1000) \cong K\ 1000^2, \text{ or}$$
$$1 \cong K\ 1000^2, \text{ and}$$
$$K \cong 1/(1000^2)$$

It follows that

$$T(100,000) \cong K\ (100,000)^2$$
$$\cong (1/1000^2)(100,000)^2$$
$$= 100^2 \text{ seconds}$$
$$\cong 2.8 \text{ hours.}$$

On the other hand, if the first sorting had been done with quick sort (with the same result), we would use $T(n) \cong K n \text{ Lg } n$, and our approximation would proceed as follows:

$$T(1000) \cong K\ 1000 \text{ Lg}(1000) \text{ or}$$
$$1 \cong K\ 1000 \text{ Lg}(1000), \text{ and}$$
$$K \cong 1/(1000 \text{ Lg}(1000))$$
$$\cong 1/(1000\ 10)$$
$$\cong 1/(10,000)$$

It follows that

$$T(100,000) \cong K\ 100,000 \text{ Lg}(100,000)$$
$$\cong (1/10,000)(100,000 \text{ Lg}(100,000))$$
$$\cong (1/10,000)(100,000\ 16.6)$$
$$\cong 166 \text{ seconds}$$
$$\cong 2.8 \text{ minutes.}$$

This hypothetical example serves to show the dramatic difference between $\theta(n^2)$ and $\theta(n \text{ Lg } n)$ as the size of the data set increases.

You should now run the lab software package and click the **Sort Timer** button. You should see a screen like the one in Figure 6.5. The **Algorithm** menu provides a choice of sort algorithms including the ones discussed so far together with some other well-known algorithms. The **Points** menu gives a choice as to the number of points to be sorted. The time it takes to do the sort is shown in the lower-right. The **Reset** button stops execution and generates a new set of data. The **Run** button executes the chosen sort algorithm on the data set. The **Pause** button temporarily stops the execution so that we can study the scatter plot. Clicking **Pause** again or **Run** resumes execution of the algorithm.

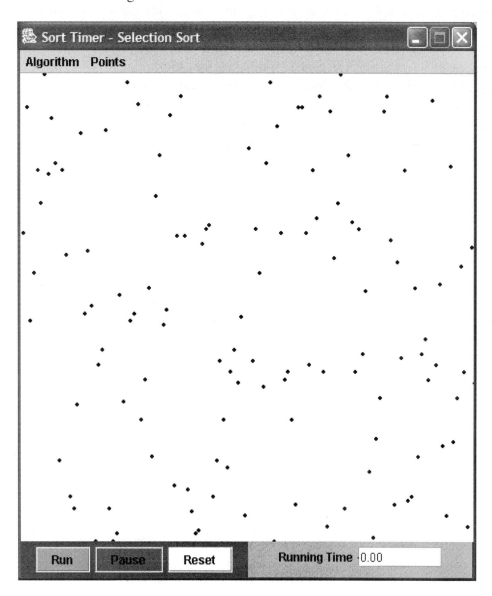

Figure 6.5 The Sort Timer screen

Exercise 6.1. Running selection sort

The selection sort algorithm is the current algorithm when the simulator starts up. From the **Points** menu, experiment with various numbers of points. Each time, click on the **Run** button and watch the scatter plot until the sort completes. Notice the sorted and unsorted sections during the run.

Exercise 6.2. Where were the sorted points originally?

Now choose enough points so that you will be able to pause the sort during the execution. Click on the **Reset** button to get a new set of data. Click on the **Run** button again, but this time click on the **Pause** button when the sorted section contains about half of the points. The scatter plot should look something like that in Figure 6.6. The following series of questions are based on this diagram. Before answering, think carefully about the details of the selection sort algorithm. Record your answers on the Worksheet.

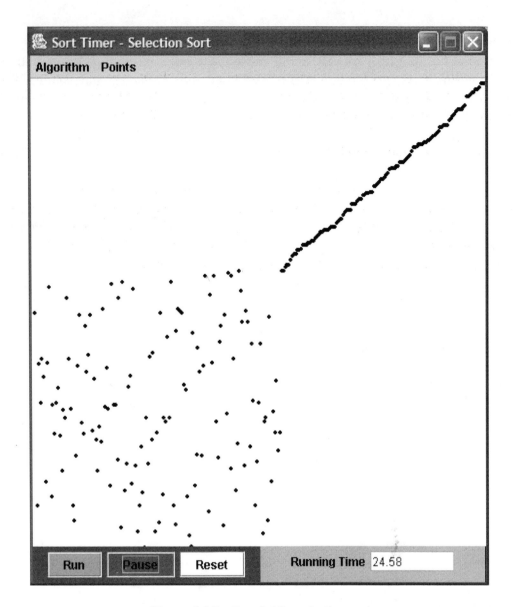

Figure 6.6 Scatter plot for selection sort

The sorted part now shows up roughly in the upper-right quadrant of the graph. Is it possible that any of these sorted points may have originated in the lower half of the graph before being "moved"? Explain your answer.

Exercise 6.3. Where were the unsorted points originally?

Is it possible that any of the points in the lower-left quadrant were originally in the lower-right quadrant? Explain your answer.

Exercise 6.4. Direction of motion

Let L mean that a point has moved to the left, and R mean that a point has moved to the right; so, LR would mean that the point has moved to the left and later moved to the right. Which of the pairs LL, LR, RL, RR are possible and which are impossible? Explain.

Exercise 6.5. Running bubble sort

Now choose the **Bubble Sort** algorithm from the **Algorithm** menu, and click on the **Reset** button. Proceed as before to watch a run or two of the algorithms. As before, on one of the runs, pause when the sorted section contains about half of the points (see Figure 6.7). The next series of questions refer to this figure. Give your answers on the Worksheet.

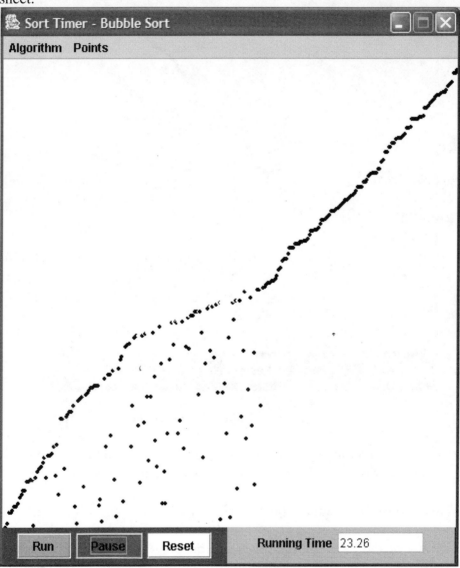

Figure 6.7 Scatter plot for bubble sort

Exercise 6.6. Where did the lower-right points go?

Which part of the graph now contains the points that were originally in the lower-right section of the graph? Explain your answer.

Exercise 6.7. Some moved, but aren't sorted

Some points have moved to the right, but are not yet in the sorted section. Can you tell where they are located?

Exercise 6.8. Contrasting selection and bubble

Discuss differences you note between the scatter plots for selection sort and bubble sort. Explain these differences in terms of the algorithms. In other words, if you were given a scatter plot of a partially completed sort, how could you tell whether it was selection sort or bubble sort?

Exercise 6.9. Direction of motion

Which of the pairs LL, LR, RL, RR are possible and which are impossible with bubble sort? Explain.

Exercise 6.10. Running quick sort

Now choose the **Quick Sort** algorithm from the **Algorithm** menu and do a few runs with different numbers of points. Notice the patterns that are formed. Also, notice approximately how long the runs take. Choose a number of points that will allow you to pause during the run. Now do a run and pause at approximately one fourth of the time for completion; if the entire run takes about 16 seconds, then pause at about 4 seconds. You should have a graph something like that in Figure 6.8. Notice the "boxes" of points arranged diagonally from lower-left to upper-right. Your graph may have a different number of boxes and may have a different sized line formed at the left. The next series of questions will refer to this figure. Give your answers on the Worksheet.

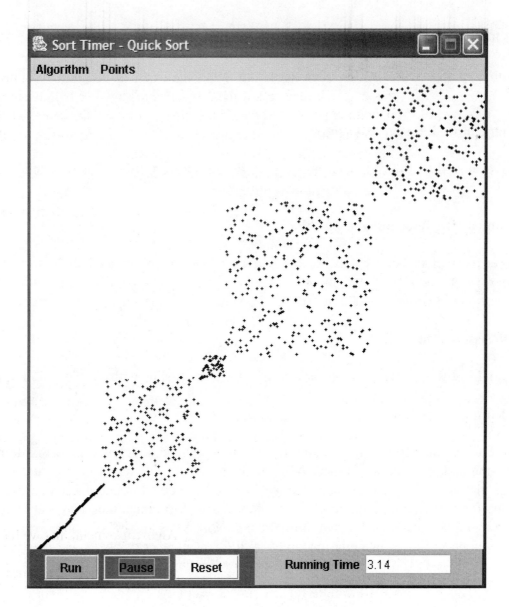

Figure 6.8 Scatter plot for quick sort

Exercise 6.11. Pattern formed by quick sort

How many "boxes" of points seem to be in the figure? Indicate the box that you think the algorithm is sorting. Indicate the box that you think will be sorted next.

Exercise 6.12. Timing selection sort

Choose the **Selection Sort** algorithm from the **Algorithm** menu and experiment to find the least number of points that will require at least 3 seconds to sort. Let N represent this number of points. Now do three or four runs with N points and record the times. Compute the average and use the average and the fact that selection sort is $\theta(n^2)$ to predict how long it will take to sort 2N points. Now test your predictions by doing actual runs. How well did this work out? Use the Worksheet for your answers.

Exercise 6.13. Timing bubble sort

Choose the **Bubble Sort** algorithm from the **Algorithm** menu and experiment with the number of points to find the smallest number of points that will require at least 3 seconds to sort. Let N indicate this number of points. Now do three or four runs with N points and record the times. Compute the average time and use the average and the fact that bubble sort is $\theta(n^2)$ to predict how long it will take to sort twice this number of points (2N points). Always show your work. For a short cut, if an algorithm is $\theta(n^2)$, then doubling the size of the data set should multiply the time by 4. Now do a couple of runs with 2N points to test your prediction. How well did the predictions work out? Compare this with the naive conjecture that doubling the data set would double the work to be done. Keep in mind that our estimates are only rough predictions. Record your answers on the Worksheet.

Exercise 6.14. Timing insertion sort

Repeat Exercise 6.13, only using insertion sort instead of bubble sort. Insertion sort is also $\theta(n^2)$.

Exercise 6.15. Timing quick sort

Choose the **Quick Sort** algorithm from the **Algorithm** menu and experiment to find the least number of points that will require at least 3 seconds to sort. Let N represent this number of points. Now do three or four runs with N points and record the times. Compute the average and use the average and the fact that quick sort is $\theta(n \text{ Lg } n)$ to predict how long it will take to sort 2N points and 4N points. Now test your predictions by doing actual runs. How well did this work out? Use the Worksheet for your answers.

Exercise 6.16. A mystery sort

There are two sort algorithms, merge sort and heap sort, under the **Algorithm** menu that we have not studied. Choose one of these algorithms and find the least number of points that requires at least 3 seconds to sort. Let N represent this number of points. Now do three runs with N points and record the times. Compute the average and make a prediction for the time for 2N points assuming first that the algorithm is $\theta(n^2)$. Then make a prediction for 2N points assuming that the algorithm is $\theta(n \text{ Lg } n)$. Now do a couple of runs with 2N points and record the times. Based on the results of this experiment, do you think the algorithm is probably $\theta(n^2)$ or $\theta(n \text{ Lg } n)$? Use the Worksheet for your answers

Worksheet
Lab Experience 6
Sort Timing

Name: _____

Course: _____

Exercise 6.2. Where were the sorted points originally?

Could any of the sorted points have originated in the lower half of the graph?

Explain why or why not:

Exercise 6.3. Where were the unsorted points originally?

Could any of the points in the lower-left quadrant have originated in the lower-right?

Explain why or why not:

Exercise 6.4. Direction of motion

Is LL possible (could a point move left and then move left again)?

Explain why or why not:

Is LR possible?

Explain:

Is RL possible?

Explain:

Is RR possible?

Explain:

Exercise 6.6. Where did the lower-right points go?

Where are the points that were originally in the lower-right?

Explain:

Exercise 6.7. Some moved, but aren't sorted

Some points have moved to the right, but are not yet in the sorted section. On the graph below, draw a line around the set of points that you think fit this description.

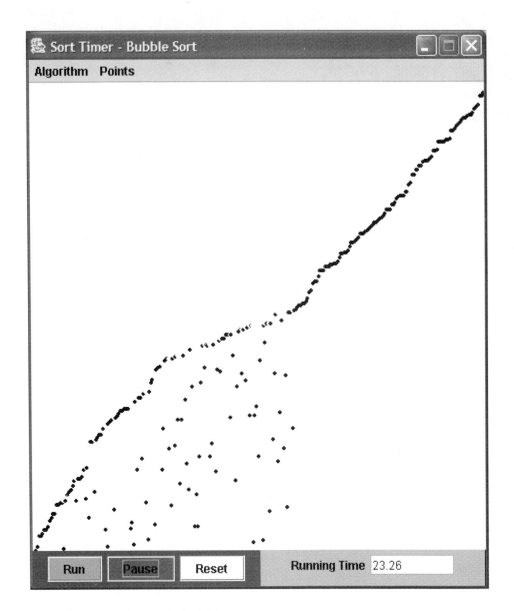

Exercise 6.8. Contrasting selection and bubble

Describe a difference between a selection sort scatter plot and a bubble sort scatter plot:

Explain this difference in terms of the steps the algorithms perform:

Exercise 6.9. Direction of motion

Is LL possible for bubble sort?

Explain why or why not:

Is LR possible?

Explain:

Is RL possible?

Explain:

Is RR possible?

Explain:

Exercise 6.11. Pattern formed by quick sort

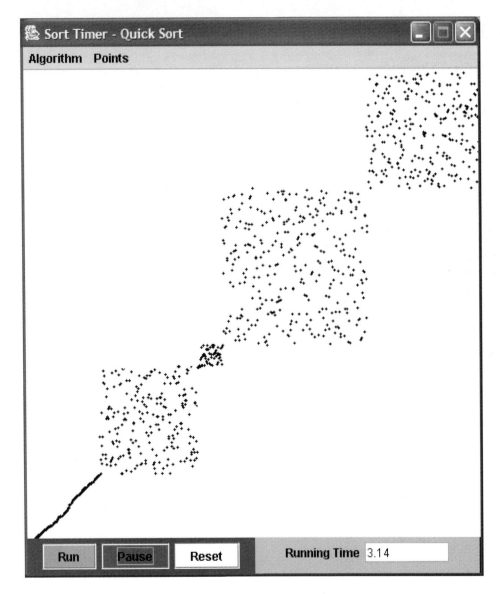

How many "boxes" of points do there seem to be in the figure?

Indicate the box that you think the algorithm is sorting by putting the number 1 above the box.

Indicate the box that you think will be sorted next by putting the number 2 above the box.

Exercise 6.12. Timing selection sort

Smallest number of points that requires 3 seconds (N points):

Give times for 3 runs with N points:

Average time:

Estimate of time for 2N points:

Give times for 2 runs with 2N points:

Do you think the theoretical estimate was fairly accurate or not?

Exercise 6.13. Timing bubble sort

Smallest number of points that requires 3 seconds (N points):

Give times for 3 runs with N points:

Average time:

Estimate of time for 2N points (show computations):

Give times for 2 runs with 2N points:

Do you think the theoretical estimate was fairly accurate or not?

How well would doubling the time for N points work as a prediction for 2N points?

Exercise 6.14. Timing insertion sort

Smallest number of points that requires 3 seconds (N points):

Give times for 3 runs with N points:

Average time:

Estimate of time for 2N points:

Give times for 2 runs with 2N points:

Do you think the theoretical estimate was fairly accurate or not?

How well would doubling the time for N points work as a prediction for 2N points?

Exercise 6.15. Timing quick sort

Smallest number of points that requires 3 seconds (N points):

Give times for 3 runs with N points:

Average time:

Estimate of time for 2N points:

Give times for 2 runs with 2N points:

Estimate of time for 4N points:

Give times for 2 runs with 4N points:

Do you think the theoretical estimate was fairly accurate or not?

Exercise 6.16. A mystery sort

Which algorithm did you choose?

Smallest number of points that requires 3 seconds (N points):

Give times for 3 runs with N points:

Average time:

Estimate of time for 2N points assuming algorithm is $\theta(n2)$:

Estimate of time for 2N points assuming algorithm is $\theta(n\ Lg\ n)$:

Give times for 2 runs with 2N points:

What do you believe is the most likely classification for this algorithm?

Lab Experience 7

Logic Circuits (A)

Objectives

- Work with a logic circuit simulator to create and test simple logic circuits
- Test the circuits by providing a full suite of inputs and checking that outputs are correct
- Give truth tables for circuits showing complete functionality of the circuits

Background

Figure 7.1 shows the various circuit components you will use in the exercises.

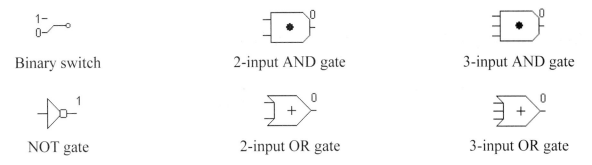

Binary switch	2-input AND gate	3-input AND gate

NOT gate	2-input OR gate	3-input OR gate

Figure 7.1 The circuit components

The small lines at the left of each gate are the connection points for input lines to the gate. Only one input line can be connected to each input connection point. The line attached to the right of the gate is the connection point for output lines from the gate. You may connect as many output lines to this point as you like. The number at the upper-right of a gate indicates the value of the output of the gate. In the case of the 2-input AND gate, this value would change to 1 if the two input lines to the gate have values of 1. Notice the 3-input AND gate. This gate takes three input lines and produces an output of 1 only if all three inputs have values of 1. This gate could be replaced by two 2-input AND gates, but provides for simpler circuit diagrams. The binary switch provides a single output line with the current value of the switch. The value of the switch changes from 0 to 1 or 1 to 0 when we click on the switch.

You should now run the lab software package and click the **Logic Circuits** button.

The example circuit

In this exercise, you will work with a circuit that has already been constructed. To get started, select **Open** under the **File** menu and then choose the file **example.cir**. You should now see the circuit shown in Figure 7.2. Notice that both switches are originally in the 0 position.

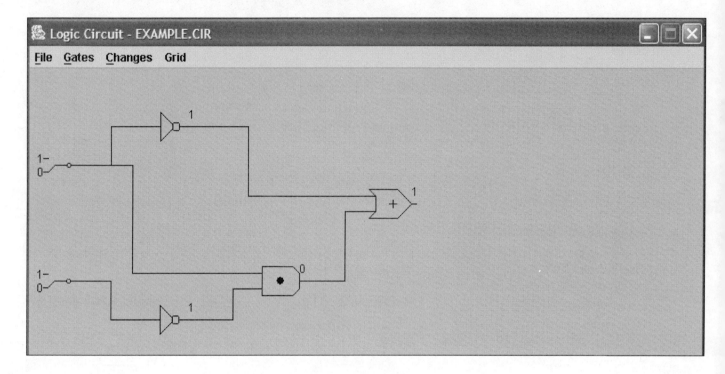

Figure 7.2 The example circuit

The output value of the upper NOT gate is 1 since its input value from the upper switch is 0. The output value of the lower NOT gate is 1 since its input from the lower switch is 0. The input values to the AND gate are 0 from the upper switch and 1 from the lower NOT gate. Thus, the output value of the AND gate is 0. The inputs to the OR gate are 1 from the upper NOT gate and 0 from the AND gate. The output value of the OR gate is therefore 1. This would be considered the output for the circuit for this setting of the two switches.

To set the values of the switches, select **Set Switch** from the **Changes** menu, as shown in Figure 7.3.

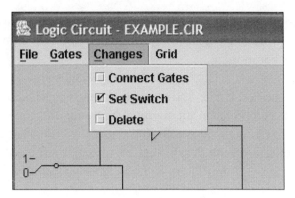

Figure 7.3 Preparing to set switches

Now you can change or toggle the value on any switch by clicking on it.

Exercise 7.1. Truth table for the example circuit

Using A and B to denote the switches, on the Worksheet, fill in the truth table for the circuit by trying each setting of the switches and recording the output value of the circuit.

Exercise 7.2. A slight change in the example circuit

If you inadvertently made any changes to the example circuit, reload **example.cir**. Now we will experiment with changing the OR gate to an AND gate. First, it will help to keep track of where the gates are by locating them within a rectangular grid. To display the grid, select **On** from the **Grid** menu. Then choose **Delete** from the **Changes** menu. Now you can delete any gate or switch in your circuit by clicking on it. Click on the OR gate. The gate together with the lines coming into it should disappear.

Next, select **And Gate** from the **Gates** menu. Click in the area previously occupied by the OR gate. You should see an AND gate appear in the grid cell where you clicked.

Choose **Connect Gates** from the **Changes** menu. Now you can connect any gates and switches in the circuit, as long as connections between them are allowed. Here are some rules of thumb for connecting components:

1. The component sending the output signal must be to the left of the component receiving the input signal. Components can only be connected in left-to-right order.

2. Always start by selecting the component that sends the output (this component should be the one to the left). When you select this component, its color changes to red and remains that color until you have successfully connected it to a receiver component.

3. Finish by selecting the desired receiver component. If that component has an available input connector, the computer will draw a new line between the two components. If no change occurs, select a different receiver component.

In the current example, click on the NOT gate and then on the new AND gate. Now connect the lower AND gate to the new AND gate by first clicking on the lower AND gate and then clicking on the new AND gate. When you are finished editing the circuit, you can hide the grid by choosing **On** from the **Grid** menu. Fill in the truth table for the resulting circuit on the Worksheet by observing the output for each setting of the input switches. In case you might need this circuit later, you can save it, say as **example2.cir**, by taking the **Save** option under the **File** menu.

Exercise 7.3. Another change

Now, starting with the circuit which resulted from Exercise 7.2, change the original AND gate to an OR gate, and fill in the truth table for the resulting circuit. You might want to save this circuit as Example3.cir.

Exercise 7.4. A simpler version of the example circuit

There is a simpler circuit that will produce the same outputs as the demo circuit, the original Example.cir. Such a circuit can be made with a single 2-input AND gate and a single NOT gate. Choose **New** from the **File** menu and elect to delete the current circuit. The entire circuit should disappear. Display the grid. Choose **Switch** from the **Gates** menu, and place switches in the first and third cells of the leftmost column in the grid. Finally, drop an AND gate and a NOT gate into grid cells somewhere to the right of the switches, and hide the grid. Now experiment with various ways of connecting the components until you find a circuit giving the same truth table as the original example circuit. To try different ways of connecting the gates, you can delete lines and then reconnect the gates and switches. Draw the simpler circuit on the Worksheet.

Exercise 7.5. A one-bit equality circuit

The one-bit equality circuit outputs a 1 when both of its inputs are the same and a 0 otherwise. The design of this circuit is discussed in Section 4.4.3 of the text, and the resulting circuit is shown in Figure 7.4 below. Construct and test such a circuit with the simulator. Give the output values in the truth table on the Worksheet.

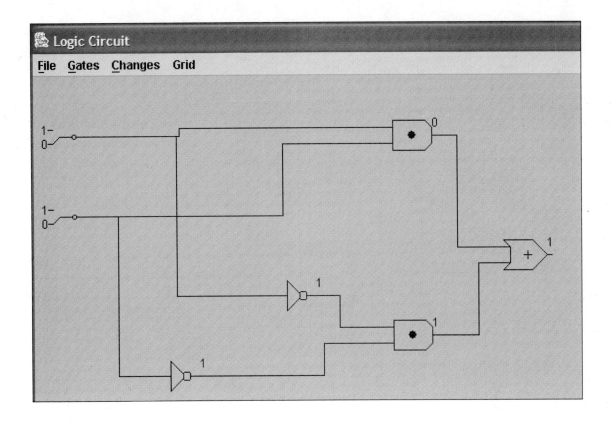

Figure 7.4 One-bit equality circuit

Worksheet
Lab Experience 7
Logic Circuits (A)

Name: _____

Course: _____

Exercise 7.1. Truth table for the example circuit

A	B	Output Value
0	0	
0	1	
1	0	
1	1	

Exercise 7.2. A slight change in the example circuit

A	B	Output Value
0	0	
0	1	
1	0	
1	1	

Exercise 7.3. Another change

A	B	Output Value
0	0	
0	1	
1	0	
1	1	

Exercise 7.4. A simpler version of the example circuit

Diagram of the simpler circuit:

Exercise 7.5. A one-bit equality circuit

A	B	Output Value
0	0	
0	1	
1	0	
1	1	

Lab Experience 8

Logic Circuits (B)

Objectives

- Practice giving circuit specifications using a truth table to show desired outputs for the various inputs
- Use the sum-of-products algorithm presented in Chapter 4 of the text to give Boolean expressions meeting the truth table specifications
- Use the lab software to construct and test the circuits corresponding to the Boolean expressions
- Understand how computer scientists can use tools of logic and mathematics to design some components of computer hardware

Exercise 8.1. Sum-of-products for the example circuit

Starting with the truth table of Exercise 7.1 of the lab manual and given below, apply the sum-of-products algorithm to obtain a Boolean expression for another circuit that would provide the same outputs as the example circuit. Then construct the new circuit with the simulator. Note how many more gates would be required for this circuit than appear in the original example circuit. After you have tested the circuit, give the Boolean expression and make a neat drawing of the circuit on the Worksheet.

A	B	Output Value
0	0	1
0	1	1
1	0	1
1	1	0

$$\overline{A} \cdot \overline{B} + \overline{A} \cdot B + A \cdot \overline{B} = C$$

Exercise 8.2. Two-input parity bit circuit

An *odd parity bit* (see Exercise 20 of Chapter 4 of the text) is an extra bit, attached to the end of a string of bits, which is set to 1 or 0 in such a way that the entire string, including the parity bit, contains an odd number of 1's. For example, if the original string of bits is 01101010, then the parity bit should be a 1, yielding the result 011010101 with an odd number of 1's. If the original string is 100110, the parity bit is 0

77

since the original string already has an odd number of 1's. In this exercise, design and test a circuit that produces as its output value the correct odd parity bit to accompany two one-bit input values. In other words, the original string has two bits, one bit for each input value. The final string will have three bits consisting of the two one-bit inputs and the one-bit output from the circuit. Thus the output value should be 1 in the case where both inputs are 0 and in the case where both inputs are 1. Fill in the truth table on the Worksheet, apply the sum-of-products algorithm to derive the Boolean expression, construct the circuit, and finally test it. Give the Boolean expression and a neat drawing of the circuit on the Worksheet.

Exercise 8.3. Three-input parity bit circuit

Following the design technique of the first two exercises, construct and test a three-bit parity circuit.

Exercise 8.4. Bits as operation codes

Later in the course, you will study in some depth how certain bits in computer instructions are used as codes to let the computer know which operation to perform. For example, one code might indicate that an addition should be performed, while another code might indicate that a compare for equality should be performed. In this exercise, you will design, construct, and test a circuit that performs this kind of function. Your circuit will have three inputs and a single output. The first two inputs are used as codes to indicate what should be done to the third input to produce the output. There are four possibilities for the two-bit codes, 00, 01, 10, and 11. We'll use the codes as follows:

(1)   If the first two input values are 0 (code 00), the output should be 0, no matter what the third input is. Here the function of the circuit becomes a set-to-zero function on the third input.

(2)   If the first input is 0 and the second is 1 (code 01), the output should be the same as the third input. The function of the circuit is the identity function on the third input.

(3)   If the first input is 1 and the second is 0 (code 10), the output should be the negation of the third input.

(4)   If the first two inputs are 1 (code 11), the output should be 1 no matter what the third input is. The function is a set-to-one operation.

Make a truth table that gives the appropriate output values according to this discussion, write the corresponding Boolean expression, construct the circuit with the simulator, and test the circuit by checking the output values for each setting of the switches.

Worksheet
Lab Experience 8
Logic Circuits (B)

Name: _____

Course: _____

Exercise 8.1. Sum-of-products for the example circuit

Boolean expression for new version of the example circuit:

Circuit diagram for the new version of the example circuit:

Exercise 8.2. Two-input parity bit circuit

A	B	Odd Parity Bit
0	0	
0	1	
1	0	
1	1	

Boolean expression of two-input parity circuit:

Circuit diagram for two-input parity circuit:

Exercise 8.3. Three-input parity bit circuit

A	B	C	Odd Parity Bit
0	0	0	
0	0	1	
0	1	0	
0	1	1	
1	0	0	
1	0	1	
1	1	0	
1	1	1	

Boolean expression of three-input parity circuit:

Circuit diagram for three-input parity circuit:

Exercise 8.4. Bits as operation codes

A (code bit 1)	B (code bit 2)	C	Result
0	0	0	
0	0	1	
0	1	0	
0	1	1	
1	0	0	
1	0	1	
1	1	0	
1	1	1	

Boolean expression:

Circuit diagram:

Lab Experience 9

von Neumann Machines

Objectives

- Work with the simulator to understand the operation of a simple Von Neumann machine
- Observe the behavior of data memory and various registers as you step through program instructions
- Work with a machine language to see what programming would be like without advances provided by modern programming languages

In this lab experience, you will be placed in much the same position as that of the first computer programmers, who had to enter each machine language instruction by hand. By giving you exposure to a "bare machine," we hope that you will appreciate the extent to which the programming process becomes automated in later lab sections.

Background

As you learned in Chapter 5 of the text, von Neumann machines have a finite amount of memory for storing program instructions and data. They also have a collection of registers for quickly locating important data, such as the address of the next instruction in memory or the contents of the instruction about to be executed. The instructions and data in a von Neumann machine are represented as strings of binary digits—machine code in the conventional sense. Finally, each instruction is executed in the order in which it is found in memory, unless a jump instruction causes control to branch around a series of instructions to some other location in memory.

The architecture and instruction set of our machine closely resemble those described in Chapter 5 of the text. Each instruction consists of two parts: a four-bit opcode that represents the operation to be performed, and a twelve-bit address field that represents the address of the operand. The sixteen binary opcodes and their meanings are shown in the following table.

Numeric code	Meaning
0000	load x x → R
0001	store x R → x
0010	clear x 0 → x
0011	add x R+x → R
0100	increment x x+1 → x
0101	subtract x R-x → R
0110	decrement x x-1 → x
0111	compare x if x>R then 100 → CCR elseif x<R then 001 → CCR elseif x=R then 010 → CCR
1000	jump x goto x
1001	jumpgt x goto x if CCR=100
1010	jumpeq x goto x if CCR=010
1011	jumplt x goto x if CCR=001
1100	jumpneq x goto x if CCR<>010
1101	in x store input in x
1110	out x output x
1111	halt

The memory of the machine contains 4096 (exactly 4K) cells of memory. Each cell contains 16 bits. If a cell contains a machine language instruction, then the leftmost four bits represent the opcode, and the remaining twelve bits represent the address of the operand. If a cell contains a machine language datum, then the leftmost bit represents the sign bit of a 15-bit integer (0 = '+', 1 = '-'), and the remaining 15 bits represent the integer's absolute value.

At the level of machine code, data and instructions all look the same. For example, suppose that the contents of the tenth cell in memory is the binary string '1000000000000111.' If we view this string as an instruction, the leftmost four bits ('1000') represent the opcode for **jump**, while the remaining twelve bits represent the address of the operand (the destination of the jump). Put simply, the instruction says "jump to location number 7" (actually, to the eighth cell in memory, because we start at location zero). If we view this string as data, however, we have a 16-bit signed integer value, namely, -7 (the leftmost bit denotes '-', while the remaining 15 bits represent 7).

To run the von Neumann machine simulator, click **von Neumann Machine** on the lab software menu. The von Neumann machine is displayed as a group of several panes on the screen (see Figure 9.1):

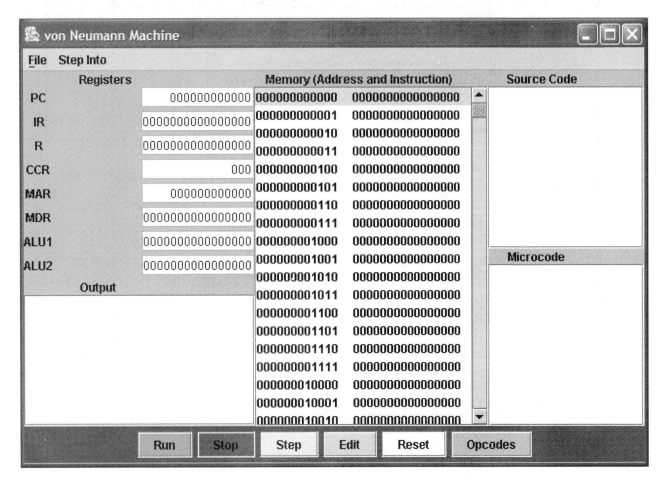

Figure 9.1 von Neumann machine simulator

In the exercises that follow, you will not be asked to enter an entire machine language program by hand. Instead, you will load some sample programs provided with the lab software, and run them to observe their behavior.

Exercise 9.1. Adding two numbers and displaying the result

Begin by selecting **Open** from the **File** menu. You should search for the file **Example1.mac** in the **Examples** folder, and then load it by clicking **OK**. If all goes well, you should see the first machine language program in memory (see Figure 9.2).

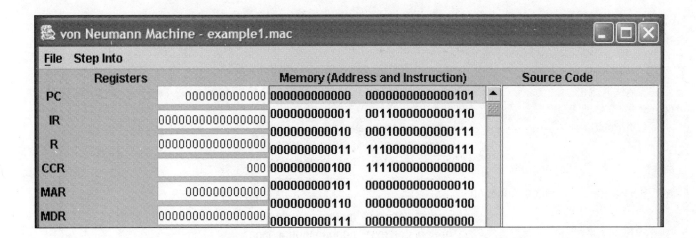

Figure 9.2 Example1.mac loaded into memory

Notice that the first machine language instruction in memory is shaded. Let's interpret this instruction. The opcode is 0000, which indicates a load instruction. The address is 000000000101 which is binary for decimal 5. Thus the instruction should load the value stored at address 5 into the register R. Memory location 5 contains a binary 2. So an appropriate interpretation for this instruction would be "The value 2 stored in location 5 is to be loaded into R." Now on the Worksheet copy down the binary form of this instruction and the interpretation of what the instruction should do when executed. Next, click the **Step** button. This will execute the first instruction. Note what happens to the contents of the registers, and that the next instruction is now shaded. Now repeat the process of writing down the instruction and your interpretation of it, and stepping through it, until a message box appears that signals the halting of the program. If you need help, look in Table 9.1, or click on the **Opcodes** button. On the Worksheet, give the main function of the program. Tell whether or not there is any output in the output window.

Exercise 9.2. Editing memory to use different data

Based on what you saw in the first exercise, where are the data for the program located? On the Worksheet, give the memory addresses where the data (as opposed to the instructions) are located. You will now run the program again with different data. To place a new datum in a memory cell, select the desired cell and click the **Edit** button. Do that now for the first **data** cell of the program. You should see a cell editor box that displays the current contents of the cell (Figure 9.3).

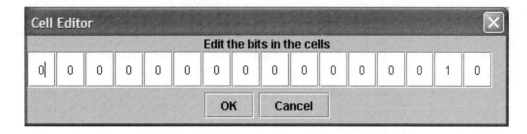

Figure 9.3 Entering new data into memory cell

Enter the number 7 in binary form. Then move to the next data cell and enter the number 8 in binary form. Finally, click the **Reset** button and run the program by clicking **Run** this time. Did you receive the expected output? Indicate the output on the Worksheet.

Exercise 9.3. Getting data from the user

A better way to test programs with different data is to allow the user to enter the data during program execution. Moreover, it would be nice if the user could enter data in a user-friendly manner, with decimal notation for integer values. Load the file **Example2.mac** from the **Examples** folder. Write down your interpretations of the first three instructions in the Worksheet. Now step through the program. When you are prompted for input data, enter binary values for decimal values such as 34 and 76.

Exercise 9.4. Making choices by comparison and jump

You will recall from the discussion of algorithms in the first three chapters of the text that we can test data for certain properties and make a decision about which statements to execute as a result of what we find. Suppose we want to display the smaller of two input values. The algorithm might compare the two numbers and, if the first is smaller than the second, then display the first; otherwise, the algorithm will display the second. To observe this algorithm as a machine language program, load the file **Example3.mac** from the **Examples** folder. Run the program a couple of times with different input values to get a sense that it does what it is supposed to do. For each of the instructions up to the halt instruction, write down the instruction and your interpretation of the instruction. Then reset and step through the execution of the program using the binary value for 5 for the first input and the binary value for 7 for the second input. Record on the Worksheet the address of the instruction being executed and the values stored in the top four registers (pc, ir, r and ccr) immediately after executing the instruction. What happened to the **ccr** register after the comparison took place? Did the machine execute one **jump** instruction, or two? Now reset and repeat the procedure by reversing the order of the two input values.

Exercise 9.5. Looping by comparison and jump

Recall from the text that many algorithms require that a block of instructions be run repeatedly, until a condition becomes true (you have been doing this yourself in the previous exercises—interpreting and stepping through an instruction, until the program halts). For example, we might want to input an arbitrary number of numbers and compute and display their average. We would first input the number of numbers expected, save this value in an extra memory location for a counter, and set a running total to zero. Then, we would input a number, add it to the running total, and subtract one from the counter, until the counter became zero. After the loop was finished, we would divide the total by the number of numbers expected and display the result.

A simpler algorithm that illustrates looping in machine language is in the file **Example4.mac**. Load that program now. The algorithm displays all of the integer values between an input value and 1 inclusive, assuming that the input value is greater than 0. Run the program once to verify that this is the case. Then step through it to observe the behavior of the loop more closely. Write down your interpretation of each instruction as you make the first pass through the loop. What would happen if the input value were zero? What would happen if the input value were a negative number?

Exercise 9.6. An error: integer overflow

We will take your data from Exercise 1 and put an error into it to illustrate an important point about von Neumann machines. Load the file **Example1.mac**. Edit either of the data cells in the program, so that the value in one of them is '0111111111111111.' This is the largest positive integer that can be represented by 16-bit signed magnitude notation. What do you suppose should happen when the machine tries to add a positive number to this value? The best way to see is to run the program. Be sure that the other number is greater than zero (1 will do just fine). The program should halt at the addition instruction with an error message. This is an example of an error for integer overflow. The nice thing about this error is that the machine finds it for you and tells you exactly what it is and where it occurs. Integer overflow occurs when the machine cannot represent the result of an arithmetic calculation in the given amount of memory. In the case of our machine, the magnitude or absolute value of the number must not exceed 32767.

Exercise 9.7. Observing fetch, decode, and execute

Recall from Chapter 5 that stepping through each machine language instruction involves three phases: fetch, decode, and execute. The first two phases, fetch and decode, are the same for every instruction. Briefly, fetch copies the address from the program counter (PC) to the memory address register (MAR). This address is then used to fetch the contents of the instruction, which is placed in the memory data register (MDR). The instruction is copied from the MDR to the instruction register (IR). Finally, the address in the PC is incremented by 1. The decode phase extracts the four-bit opcode from the instruction in the IR, and sends it to the instruction decoder. The third phase, execute, is different for each instruction. For example, executing the instruction load x consists of three steps: (1) extract the address of x from the IR and copy it to the MAR; (2) fetch the contents at this address and copy it into the MDR; and (3) copy the contents of the MDR into the data register (R). To observe the fetch/decode/execute cycle, load the file **Example1.mac** into memory and select **On** from the **Step Into** menu (see Figure 9.4).

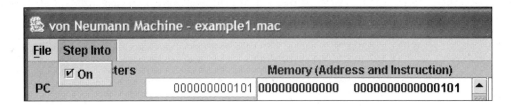

Figure 9.4 Turning on Step Into

As long as this item is checked, you will be able to step through a program but not run it. As you step into each instruction in memory, a description of the fetch cycle pops up in the pane at the lower-right of the window. Each click of the Step button now moves the black bar down through the instructions in the fetch cycle. Note the changes in the MAR and MDR as you go. When you get to the execute phase, you may see changes to the ALU registers as well. If you wish to turn off this feature so that you can step through a program more quickly or run it, just select **On** from **Step Into** again.

Worksheet
Lab Experience 9
von Neumann Machines

Name: _____

Course: _____

Exercise 9.1. Adding two numbers and displaying the result

Instruction	Interpretation

Main function of the program:

Any output in output window:

Exercise 9.2. Editing memory to use different data

Output of run with new data:

Exercise 9.3. Getting data from the user

Instruction	Interpretation

Exercise 9.4. Making choices by comparison and jump

Address	Instruction	Interpretation
0		
1		
2		
3		
4		
5		
6		

Address	Instruction	Interpretation
7		
8		

Stepping with first input value 5 and second input value 7:

Address	pc	ir	r	ccr

What happened to the value in ccr?

How many jumps were executed?

Stepping with first input value 7 and second input value 5:

Address	pc	ir	r	ccr

What happened to the value in ccr?

How many jumps were executed?

Exercise 9.5. Looping by comparison and jump

Address	Instruction	Interpretation
0		
1		
2		
3		
4		
5		
6		
7		
8		

Lab Experience 10

Assembly Language Programming

Objectives

- Experience a brief introduction to assembly language programming
- Use the lab software to see how assembly language programs are translated into machine language

Background

In the previous lab experience, you became acquainted with the structure and function of a simple von Neumann machine. You also experienced some of the same difficulties that the first programmers had in programming in machine language. You would probably agree that the solution of even a simple problem such as adding two numbers together and displaying the result required a great deal of thinking and planning. The problem is not in knowing what has to be done, but in translating your strategy into the unfamiliar notation of the binary machine code. When it comes to solving slightly more complex problems, like using addition to multiply two numbers, it helped the first programmers to write out the solution in a low-level pseudo code, and then translate this to the machine code. This technique simplified the programming process, but they still had to do the translation by hand. Even though the translation from the lower-level pseudo code to the machine code was fairly simple and straightforward, it was still prone to human error (typing in the wrong machine address for an instruction or data label, or typing in the wrong numeric opcode for the name of an operation).

It turns out that the process of translating from a low-level pseudo code to machine code is so simple and mechanical that a computer professional can write a program to do that for us. Then we just enter our program in the low-level pseudo code and the translator converts it to an equivalent machine language program. The low-level pseudo code is called *assembly language*, and the translator is called an *assembler*.

As you will recall from Chapter 6 of the text, the advantages of programming in assembly language instead of machine code are obvious:

1. You can work with mnemonic names for operations, data, and the locations of instructions, such as **add**, **result**, and **endwhile**. You no longer have to worry about figuring out or remembering the binary representations of addresses or opcodes.

95

2. The assembler can guarantee that data is kept separate from instructions in the machine code. You just enter the instructions in the assembly language program first, and then the data.

3. The assembler can catch many errors that would otherwise have been detected only at run-time. For example, it is possible to write a machine language instruction that jumps to a data location in memory. The assembler can stop the translation of your program and force you to fix this bug before the program ever runs. A list of these errors can be found at the end of this lab.

By automating the program translation process, an assembler provides a layer of virtual machine between you and the computer, thus making problem solving less tedious and more powerful.

To run the assembler, click **Assembler** on the main software menu. You will be presented with two panes (see Figure 10.1).

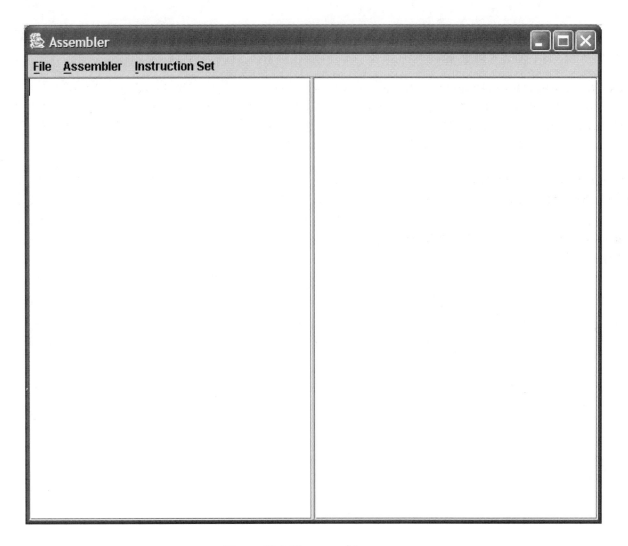

Figure 10.1 The assembler panes

The left pane is intended for the entry of assembly language source programs. The right pane is a utility area for displaying program listings during compilation, symbol tables, and object code. You also have the following menus:

1. **File**. From this menu, you can **Save** and **Open** assembly language source programs or obtain a **New** entry pane. You can also print a listing of the program after it assembles.

2. **Assembler**. From this menu, you can **Assemble** the source program, **View the symbol table** that is generated during translation (you will do this in Lab Experience 17), and **View the object code**. You can

also **Execute** the object code, which actually loads the object code into a von Neumann machine simulator.

3. **Instruction Set**. From this menu, you can view a dictionary of the instruction set.

Exercise 10.1. Adding two numbers and displaying the result

Select **Open** from the **File** menu and select the file **Example1.asm** in the **Examples** folder. Now click the **Open** button. The text of an assembly language source program should appear in the source program pane. You will recall that you loaded an equivalent machine language program in Lab Experience 9. Study the code to verify that the program will do what your machine language program did (if it ran correctly!). Then choose **Assemble** from the **Assembler** menu (see Figure 10.2). You will see a program listing appear in the utility pane. The listing is just a copy of the source program, with each line numbered for your reference. At the end of the listing, there should be a message that assembly has been completed without syntax errors.

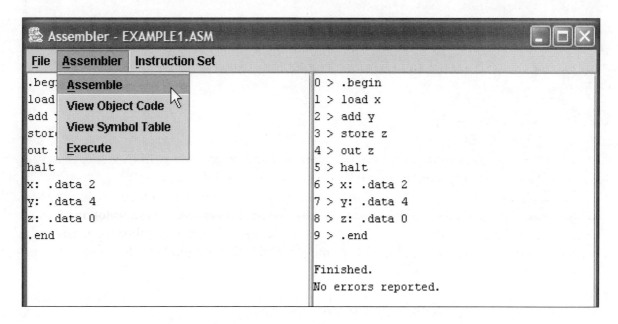

Figure 10.2 A sample assembly language program and its listing

The assembler has instantly done what you so painstakingly had to figure out yourself in the last lab section: translate some thoughts expressed in English-like code to the same thoughts expressed in machine code. To see that this is the case, select **View Object Code** from the **Assembler** menu. The machine language instructions corresponding to the source code will be displayed in the utility pane, as in Figure 10.3.

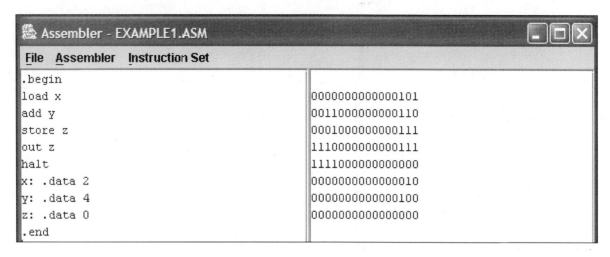

Figure 10.3 Machine code for an assembly language program

Finally, run the program by selecting **Execute** from the **Assembler** menu. A von Neumann machine simulator pops up, with the machine code of your program loaded into memory and the source code displayed in the source pane. When you run the program in the simulator (by selecting either **Run** or **Step**), the current instruction is selected in both forms of the program. Run the program and indicate the output on the Worksheet.

Exercise 10.2. Some syntax errors

You will typically begin by entering a source program by hand or opening it from a file. **Assemble** is the only option available from the **Assembler** menu at this point. During assembly, the system displays a program listing and any syntax error messages in the utility pane. Each line of source text is numbered in the listing for easy reference, and an error message appears more or less on the line following the line of code in which the error occurs. Assembly halts at the first error. Error detection is pretty thorough: errors are caught even at the lexical level, such as illegal labels and integer literals that are too large for 16-bit sign magnitude representation.

The assembler can generate the following syntax error messages:

```
.begin expected.
.end expected.
Illegal opcode: <symbol>
Halt does not take operand.
Wrong number of fields in instruction.
Label must end with :
Label already used: <symbol>
Undeclared data label: <symbol>
```

```
Undeclared instruction label: <symbol>
Data label already used as instruction label: <symbol>
Data directive already exists for label: <symbol>
Value must be an integer.
Number is too large.
Not enough memory for instructions.
Not enough memory for data.
```

The program that we just loaded from a file had no syntax errors. Let's put some syntax errors into it so that we can see how the assembler detects them.

a. Replace the operand **x** in the first instruction, **load x**, with the operand **a**, and reassemble the program. The assembler should discover that you forgot to provide a data declaration for **a**. The assembler forces you to keep track of all of your data and their initial values by declaring them at the bottom of the program. Correct this error before going on.

b. Replace the operator **add** with the operator **multiply** in the second instruction. The assembler should discover an unrecognized opcode. Correct this error before going on.

c. Replace the number 2 with the number 40000 in the first data declaration. Note the error detected by the assembler. Correct this error before going on.

d. Delete the space between **add** and **y** in the second instruction. Note the error detected. There must be at least one blank space or tab between an operator and its operand. Correct this error before going on.

e. Insert a blank line after the second instruction. Note the error detected. Assembly language typically has a *fixed format*, which requires an instruction to appear on each line of a program. Correct this error before going on.

f. Insert a blank space, followed by **subtract**, at the end of the second line. Note the error detected. Since the instruction has three lexical items, the assembler expects the first one to be a label ending with a colon (:). Don't correct this error yet.

g. Oblige the assembler by inserting a colon (:) after **add** (be sure that there are no blank spaces between the colon and the **d**). Note the error detected. Now change **y** to **add**. The assembler treats **subtract** as an undeclared data label, which you could remedy by declaring it at the bottom of the program.

Exercise 10.3. Making decisions in assembly language

Open the file **Example2.asm** and study the program. What does it do? Assemble and execute the program. Does it behave as expected? Modify the program so that it displays the larger of the two numbers, and test it until it behaves correctly.

Exercise 10.4. Loops in assembly language

Open the file **Example3.asm** and study the program. What does it do? Assemble and execute the program. Does it behave as expected? Modify the program so that it checks to see that the input data is greater than zero before it starts the loop. If that's not the case, the program should halt with no output.

Exercise 10.5. Larger/smaller

Write pseudocode for a program which allows the user to input two numbers (X and Y) and a code C. If the code has value 1, the program should output the larger of X and Y and otherwise output the smaller.

Now convert your pseudocode to an assembly language program. Enter the program into the lab software assembler. Assemble the program and execute it with different input data.

Exercise 10.6. Even/odd

Write pseudocode for a program which allows the user to input a positive number N. The program should output 1 if the number is odd and output 0 if the number is even. (*Hint*: keep subtracting 2 from N until ...)

Exercise 10.7. Multiplication

Our assembly language has no operator for multiplication. But multiplication can be performed by repeatedly adding one number to a running total, and reducing the other number by one, until the second number becomes zero. Write and test an assembly language program that displays the product of two input numbers.

Worksheet
Lab Experience 10
Assembly Language Programming

Name: _____

Course: _____

Exercise 10.1. Adding two numbers and displaying the result

Output from running the program:

Exercise 10.2. Some syntax errors

    a. Error message:

    b. Error message:

    c. Error message:

    d. Error message:

    e. Error message:

    f. Error message:

    g. First error message:

       Second error message:

Exercise 10.3. Making decisions in assembly language

What is the main function of Example2?

Write your program to give the larger of two numbers:

Exercise 10.4. Loops in assembly language

What is the main function of Example2?

Program:

Exercise 10.5. Larger/smaller

Program for larger/smaller:

Exercise 10.6. Even/odd

Program for even/odd:

Exercise 10.7. Multiplication

Program for multiplication:

Lab Experience 11

Networks

Objectives

- Observe the steps required to convert information to a form suitable for transmission across a network
- Discover how errors can occur during network transmissions and how they can be detected and corrected

In this laboratory experience, you explore these issues in depth using a simulator that models the transmission of messages across a wide-area computer network. [1]

Background

The transmission of packets across a computer network involves a number of steps, including encoding the information to be sent, encrypting information to prevent theft, and transmitting information from sender to receiver. Here are the steps involved in sending a message containing a sequence of characters $c_1 c_2 c_3 c_4 \ldots c_N$, as seen by the sending side:

1. Translate the next character in the message c_i into its ASCII code. ASCII (as mentioned in Chapter 4) assigns a unique integer value to each character. For example, the ASCII value for the letter A is 65, while the value for the letter B is 66.

2. Convert the ASCII value from decimal to binary. To support 256 distinct ASCII codes, we need to use 8 binary digits (bits) per character. The 8-bit binary representation of ASCII 65 (the letter A) is 01000001. The 8-bit representation of 66 (the letter B) is 01000010.

3. If encryption is being used, then we apply an encryption algorithm to the binary string produced in Step 2. Encryption is frequently used when sending messages across a network. This is to prevent the information from being read by unauthorized individuals either during transit or when it arrives at the receiving node. We will have more to say about encryption in Chapter 13 and in Lab Experience 22. In this lab we use a very simple encryption algorithm that does two things:

---

[1] The network lab simulator is based on a simulator created by John Gersting and J. J. Wassell of the Computer Science Department at the University of Hawaii at Hilo, and is used with their permission.

     a. Subtracts an integer quantity from the original binary number, and

     b. Shifts the bits in the result from Step *a* to the left or right a fixed number of places.

Let's assume that our algorithm subtracts 1 from the binary number and does no shifting. Then the encrypted string obtained from 01000001 (the character A) will be 01000000. The encrypted string obtained from 01000010 is 01000001. (Admittedly, this is a truly simplistic encryption algorithm that would not deter many hackers. However, as we mentioned above, we will demonstrate much more interesting encryption algorithms in a later lab exercise.)

4. Create a packet that contains the encrypted binary representation of the character we wish to transmit. Let's assume that each packet can contain up to two encrypted binary numbers. Their positions in the packet correspond to their positions as characters in the user's original data string. Each packet will also contain a sequence number that identifies the position of its data relative to the positions of other packets of data in the user's original string. That is, there will be a number within the packet that says "this is packet number 0," "this is packet number 1." We need this sequence number, since if a message is longer than 2 characters, it must be sent as multiple packets. These packets might take different routes across the network and not necessarily arrive in the order they were sent. The sequence number allows the message packets to be reassembled in the correct order at the receiving end. For example, assume that we are sending the 5-character message "Hello". Packet number 0 will contain the encrypted binary strings for the two characters 'H' and 'e'. Packet number 1 will contain the encrypted binary strings for the two characters 'l' and 'l'. Finally, the third and last packet, packet number 2, will contain the encrypted string for the value 'o'. (It will also contain the binary string representing NULL, or no character, in the second position.)

5. Add a **parity bit** to the end of each packet. The parity bit will be set such that the number of 1's in the whole string of bits, including the parity bit, is odd. The receiver can then check a packet's parity to determine whether the packet's data were corrupted during transmission by the change of a single bit from a 0 to a 1 or vice versa.

6. Transmit the message from the source node to the destination node.

If all the characters in the message have been sent, then we are done. If not, we go back to Step 1 and start the process all over again using the next two characters in the message.

If we assume that there can be up to eight characters in a single user message, then there may be up to four packets per message, numbered 0, 1, 2, 3, that must be sent across the network (remember, two characters per packet). Thus, each packet will require 19 bits—16 bits for the two encrypted characters, 2 bits for the sequence number (we need 2 bits to represent all numbers from 0 to 3), and 1 bit for parity. Figure 11.1 shows the first packet generated from the four-character message "ABCD".

0	0	0	1	0	0	0	0	0	0	1	0	0	0	0	0	1	0

Seq. 0   Encrypted 'A'   Encrypted 'B'   Parity bit

Figure 11.1 A packet for the letters "A" and "B" in the message "ABCD"

The receiver of a packet has some additional work to do, because errors can occur during transmission. That is, a message may be garbled or it may never arrive at all. Here are the essential steps in the transmission process as seen by the receiver:

1. If a packet is lost and never arrives, request the sender to resend it. We would know this, for example, if we received packet number 0 and packet number 2 of a message but never received packet number 1.

2. When a packet arrives at the receiver we check the parity bit. If the parity is incorrect, then the message was corrupted during transmission and we cannot use it. We must ask the sender to resend the packet, and we discard this incorrect copy.

3. If the parity bit is correct, then there were no transmission errors that we can detect, and the data fields inside the message are assumed to be valid. We decrypt the one or two binary strings in the message using the inverse of the process that encrypted them. That is, we shift the bits back to their original location and then we add back the integer value that was initially subtracted. This produces the correct binary value of the one or two characters in the message.

4. We convert the resulting binary string(s) to their correct decimal ASCII value and then convert those decimal values to their proper character representation.   .

5. We place these characters into the message in their correct places as specified by the sequence number. For example, message number 0 contains characters c_0 and c_1; message number 1 contains characters c_2 and c_3, etc. If the entire message is present, then we are done. If not, we must wait for the other pieces of the message to arrive.

This completes the description of how our network simulator works.

Exercise 11.1. Running the network simulator

Launch the network simulator by clicking the lab software's **Network Simulator** button. Enter the string "Hello" in the **Message to be sent** field and click the **Prepare** button. Now you can start sending the packets by clicking the **Send** button. This will move the contents of the first packet into the network. Avoid clicking the **Damage** or **Destroy** buttons for now. When you repeatedly click the **Move** button, the packets will move through the network and arrive in the receiver's **Packets** list. Note that packets may arrive in a different order than that in which they were sent, as shown in Figure 11.2. In this example the second packet made it through the network before the first one. This is a common occurrence in networks, and it is the reason why we need sequence numbers. It is similar to the situation where a piece of mail M_1 posted on Monday and another one M_2 posted on Tuesday arrive at the destination in the reverse order ($M_2 M_1$) from which they were sent.

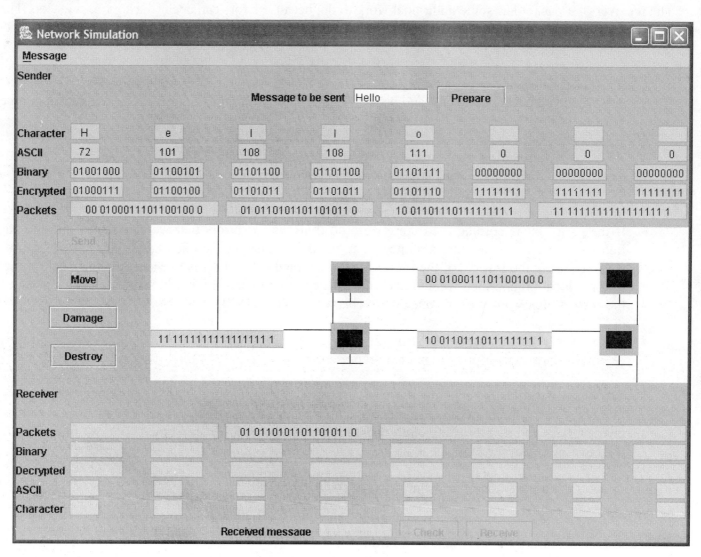

Figure 11.2 The network simulator after sending a few packets

When all of the packets have arrived, click the receiver's **Check** button to check their parity. Then click **Receive** to translate the encoded forms to the sender's original message.

Exercise 11.2. Destroying a packet

Select **New** from the **Message** menu to enter a new message. Enter your first name and click **Prepare** and then **Send**. Click **Move** once to send a second packet. Now click **Destroy**. Finally, click **Move** repeatedly until the receiver can check the packets. Click **Check** and **Fix It** and use the Worksheet to describe what happens. Can the receiver obtain the missing packet to complete the transmission?

Exercise 11.3. Damaging a packet

Repeat the steps in the previous exercise, but click the **Damage** button instead of the **Destroy** button. Describe what happens and how the receiver remedies the problem.

Exercise 11.4. Spying on the network

Resend your name by clicking **Prepare** and **Send**. Then pretend you are a hacker by selecting **Spy** from the **Message** menu. This simulates someone listening in as the message is being sent down the wire. Describe what a hacker would see. Do you think this would prevent the hacker from correctly determining the original message?

Exercise 11.5. Modifying the encryption algorithm

Select **Message/New** and enter your name. Then select **Message/Change Encryption Algorithm**. A dialog box for editing the encryption algorithm is shown in Figure 11.3.

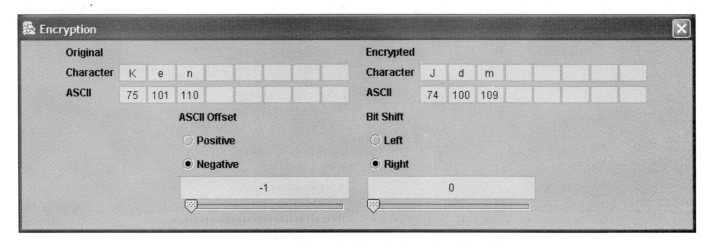

Figure 11.3 Editing the encryption algorithm

Note the default values of the ASCII offset and the bit shift. You can modify these values by selecting the desired radio button and dragging the sliders. You can add or subtract any integer value by selecting either the "Positive" or "Negative" radio button and using the slider to change the offset value. In addition, you can change both the direction and the amount of the bit shift. Reset these values to anything you want and observe how your changes affect the encrypting of the original message.

Now close the dialog box and click the **Prepare** button in the simulator. Note the changes to the encrypted binary strings. Do you think that this is a more effective encryption technique? Justify your answer. Your answer should include a description of exactly how a hacker might crack this code.

Worksheet
Lab Experience 11
Networks

Name: _____

Course: _____

Exercise 11.2. Destroying a packet

Exercise 11.3. Damaging a packet

Exercise 11.4. Spying on the network

Exercise 11.5. Modifying the encryption algorithm

Lab Experience 12

C++ Programming—Input, Output, and Control Structures

Objectives

- Work with a "high-level" language that contains powerful statements to facilitate problem solving
- Practice writing simple programs in the high-level language and using a compiler to translate them to a form that can be executed on the computer
- Learn how computer languages are defined by a very formal set of syntax rules

Background

In Chapter 5 of the text, you learned that the first programmers wrote programs directly (and, perhaps, painfully!) in machine language. In Chapter 6, you learned that a programming language translator, called an assembler, can ease the burden of writing programs. Assembly language resembles a low-level pseudo code, in which we can express algorithms in terms that are more intelligible to a human being. However, as problems get more complex, the assembly language programs that might solve them become difficult to understand as well. Even a fairly simple problem, such as writing a loop to multiply two numbers, requires us to design a solution in high-level pseudo code before translating by hand to a form resembling an assembly language program. Even if we think that our high-level design is correct, we face the additional problem of manual translation from high-level pseudo code to assembly language.

Fortunately, computer scientists have created a tool that allows you to write a program directly in a language that resembles a high-level pseudo code. The tool, called a compiler, translates programs written in a language called C++ to a form that can be executed on a machine. Actually, the compiler does not support the translation of all of the features you will find in commercially available C++; but a large subset of them is covered. The compiler supports the "procedural" subset of C++ discussed in Chapter 8 of the text. The syntax rules for our C++ appear at the end of this lab. You will see that you can solve fairly complex problems easily and quickly in C++. In the process, you should appreciate the extent to which several layers of virtual machine free you from low-level concerns and permit you to think like a human being once again.

In this lab, we examine C++ programs that have the following structure:

```
main function heading
data declarations
statements
```

117

In contrast to assembly language programs, C++ programs declare data before stating the instructions. Moreover, there are several kinds of data declarations and statements in C++. To help you keep this straight, the compiler is pretty fussy about the syntax or form of each kind of declaration and statement. You will learn the different kinds of data declarations and statements in C++ by running some example programs provided with the software. To get started, run the C++ compiler by clicking on that button on the main menu. If all goes well, you should see a window resembling the Assembler window from Lab Experience 10. Remember to keep the syntax rules and notes on our subset of C++ (at the end of this lab) handy.

Exercise 12.1. Adding two integers and displaying the result

Open the file **Example1.cpp** from the **File** menu. Compile the program by choosing **Compile** from the **Run** menu. Your window should now look like the one depicted in Figure 12.1.

```
EXAMPLE1.CPP

 File   Compiler

// File: example1.cpp              0 >  // File: example1.cpp
                                   1 >
#include <iostream.h>              2 >  #include <iostream.h>
                                   3 >
void main()                       4 >  void main()
{                                 5 >  {
    const int first = 2;          6 >      const int first = 2;
    const int second = 4;         7 >      const int second = 4;
                                   8 >
    int sum;                      9 >      int sum;
                                  10 >
    sum = first + second;        11 >      sum = first + second;
    cout << sum << endl;         12 >      cout << sum << endl;
}                                13 >  }

                                 Finished.
                                 No errors reported.
```

Figure 12.1 The C++ compiler panes

This program does exactly what the first example assembly language program did in Lab Experience 10. It takes two integer data values, adds them together, and displays their sum followed by an end of line. Note that the data are defined as constants in C++. Note also that the sum is defined as a variable. Now run the program by choosing **Execute** from the **Run** menu. The execution window shown in Figure 12.2 should pop up.

Figure 12.2 Running a C++ program

When you click **Run**, the sum of the two integers should be displayed in the window. To run the program again, click **Reset** and **Run**. Note that there are two other buttons:

- **Halt**. Use this button to stop a program, especially if it appears hung in an infinite loop.
- **Save**. Use this button to save a program's output from the window to a file.

Exercise 12.2. Dealing with syntax errors

The syntax of C++ is more complex than the syntax of assembly language. For this reason, beginning programmers frequently make syntax errors until they become acquainted with the language. When a syntax error occurs, the compiler stops and displays an informative error message near the point of error in the source program. As an example, suppose we change the first **<<** symbol in **Example1.cpp** to just the **<** symbol. When the program compiles, the error message is displayed, as shown in Figure 12.3.

```
EXAMPLE1.CPP
File  Compiler

// File: example1.cpp               0 >  // File: example1.cpp
                                    1 >
#include <iostream.h>               2 >  #include <iostream.h>
                                    3 >
void main()                         4 >  void main()
{                                   5 >  {
    const int first = 2;            6 >       const int first = 2;
    const int second = 4;           7 >       const int second = 4;
                                    8 >
    int sum;                        9 >       int sum;
                                   10 >
    sum = first + second;          11 >       sum = first + second;
    cout < sum << endl;            12 >       cout < sum << endl;
}
                                   ERROR >> << expected

                                   Finished.
                                   1 error reported.
```

Figure 12.3 A C++ syntax error message

Close the execution window from Exercise 1, and edit the output statement so that this syntax error occurs. Then fix the error and recompile. Now force another syntax error by changing the + sign to the $ symbol, and recompile. Write a short paragraph that explains the error messages in the Worksheet.

Exercise 12.3. Labeling output

Close the execution window from Exercise 1, and edit the output statement so that the output will be labeled. For example, you might say

```
cout << "The sum is " << sum << endl;
```

Recompile and execute the program, until you are satisfied with the output. Enter your changes on the Worksheet.

Exercise 12.4. Displaying the sum of two input integers

Open the file **Example2.cpp** from the **File** menu. This program is like **Example1.cpp**, but allows the user to enter the data as inputs from the keyboard. Note that the data are defined as variables rather than constants. Note also that the user is prompted for input before each input statement. Compile and execute the program. Run it with two different sets of data (remember to click **Reset** and **Run** when you just want to test a program with different data sets).

Exercise 12.5. Computing the area of a triangle

Open the file **Example3.cpp** from the **File** menu. This program computes and displays the area of a triangle, after the user has entered the height and base. Note that the height, base, and area are declared as doubles (real numbers) rather than integers. Compile and execute the program. Run it with two sets of test data.

Exercise 12.6. Converting degrees Fahrenheit to degrees centigrade

Design, code, and test a C++ program that takes degrees Fahrenheit from the user and displays the same temperature in degrees centigrade. Be sure to label the output descriptively. The formula for the conversion is

```
centigrade = (fahrenheit - 32) * 5 / 9
```

Enter your program on the Worksheet.

Exercise 12.7. The `if` statement

Open the file **Example4.cpp** from the **File** menu. You should see a program that displays the absolute value of an input number. To solve this problem, we prompt the user for a value. If the value is less than 0, then we negate it and store it back in the variable. Finally, we output the value. Note that the negation only occurs if the condition in the `if` statement is true. If the condition is false, we go on to output the value right away. This is an example of a one-way choice. Compile the program, execute it, and run it with positive and negative inputs.

Exercise 12.8. The `if...else` statement

For this exercise, you will take the preceding program and modify it so that it outputs a message that the value is positive if that is true, or negative otherwise. First, delete the output statement. Then, replace the line where the number is negated with an output statement for the message that the number is negative. Compile and run the program with positive and negative inputs. What happens? Do we get the expected output in both cases? Now return to the compiler and convert the **if** statement to a two-way decision. Insert the word **else** on the line after the **if** statement. Then, on the next line, indent one tab stop and insert an output statement for the message that the number is positive. Compile and test the program with positive and negative numbers.

Exercise 12.9. A three-way decision

It turns out that the program from the previous exercise still is not quite right. It tells us we entered a positive number when we enter a zero. Therefore, we need three possible messages, including one for the case of zero. To handle this option, we can nest the existing **if** statement in the **else** part of a higher-level **if** statement. This three-way decision should have the following form:

```
if (expression)
      statement
else if (expression)
      statement
else
      statement
```

To fix your program from the previous exercise, insert the word **else** in front of the word **if**. Then open up two lines above the first **else**, and insert an **if** statement that will handle the case where the input value is exactly zero. Compile and run the program with all three possible cases of input.

Exercise 12.10. The `while` statement

Open the file **Example5.cpp** from the **File** menu. This program illustrates the use of the *while statement* in C++. The program does the same thing as an assembly language program in Lab Experience 10: take an input integer from the user, and display all of the values from that integer down to one. This version of the while statement is known as a *count-controlled loop*. Compile the program and run it with some test values. Now suppose we wanted to display the values in ascending order. Modify the current program so that this is the result.

Exercise 12.11. Accumulating a sum

Modify the program from the previous exercise, so that it displays just the sum of all of the numbers from one to the input number. Be sure to test your program with several inputs.

Exercise 12.12. Accumulating a sum of a series of input values

Modify the program from the previous exercise, so that it displays the sum of a series of input numbers. You should prompt the user for the number of input numbers to be entered, and use this number as your loop counter.

Exercise 12.13. Accumulating a sum of absolute values

Modify the program from the previous exercise, so that it displays the sum of absolute values of a series of input numbers. That is, it should display the same result whether the input values are negative or positive.

Syntax Rules of C++ as Covered in Labs 12-14

We use an extended Backus-Naur grammar to define the subset of C++ used in labs 12-14. This grammar has three kinds of symbols:

1. **Terminal symbols**. These symbols are enclosed in double quotes. Examples are "+" and "main". These symbols are reserved words and operator symbols, and make up the vocabulary of the language.
2. **Non-terminal symbols**. These symbols designate phrases in the language that must be defined further. Examples are `functionCall` and `constantDeclaration`.
3. **Metasymbols**. The grammar uses these symbols to form rules. The metasymbols appear in the following table:

Metasymbol	Use in a rule
=	Means is defined as.
|	Separates alternative choices.
{ }	Encloses items that can appear zero or more times.
[ ]	Encloses an optional item.
( )	Encloses items that should be grouped as a unit.

The rules are formed by placing the defined symbol to the left and its definition to the right of the **=** symbol. For example, the rule

```
expression = simpleExpression [ relationalOperator simpleExpression ]
```

is read as "An expression is defined as a simple expression, which may or may not be followed by a relational operator and a simple expression." An example of an expression in a C++ program is **x >= y**.

The rule

```
simpleExpression = term { addingOperator term }
```

is read as "A simple expression is defined as a term, followed by zero or more adding operators and terms." An example of a simple expression in a C++ program is **x + y - z**.

As in English and other natural languages, every phrase in a C++ program must follow a syntax rule. If you have trouble understanding the compiler's syntax error messages, check the grammar and the list of error messages that follow:

```
program = { functionDeclaration } mainFunction

mainFunction = "void" "main" "(" ")" block

block = "{" { constantDeclaration } { variableDeclaration }
      { statement } "}"

constantDeclaration = "const" ( "int" | "double" ) identifier "="
      ( integer | double ) ";"

variableDeclaration = ( "int" | "double" | "char" ) identifierList ";"

identifierList = identifier [ "[" integerConstant "]" ]
 { "," identifier [ "[" integerConstant "]" ] }

integerConstant = integer | identifier

functionDeclaration = functionHeading block

functionHeading = returnType identifier "(" [ formalParameters ] ")"

returnType = "void" | "int" | "double" | "char"

formalParameters = parameterDeclaration { "," parameterDeclaration }

parameterDeclaration = ( "int" | "double" | "char" )
 identifier [ "[" "]" ]

statement = ifStatement | whileStatement | returnStatement
 | outputStatement | inputStatement | compoundStatement
 | assignmentStatement | functionCallStatement

ifStatement = "if" "(" expression ")" statement [ "else" statement ]

whileStatement = "while" "(" expression ")" statement

returnStatement = "return" expression ";"

outputStatement = "cout" "<<" outputExpression
 { "<<" outputExpression } ";"

inputStatement = "cin" ">>" identifier ";"

compoundStatement = "{" { statement } "}"
```

```
assignmentStatement = name "=" expression ";"

functionCallStatement = functionCall ";"

functionCall = identifier "(" [ actualParameters ] ")"

actualParameters = expression { "," expression }

outputExpression = "endl" | expression

expression = simpleExpression [ relationalOperator simpleExpression ]

simpleExpression = term { addingOperator term }

term = factor { multiplyingOperator factor }

factor = [ "-" | "!" ] primary

primary = integer | double | character | string
 | name | functionCall | "(" expression ")"

name = identifier [ "[" expression "]" ]

relationalOperator = "==" | "!=" | ">" | "<" | ">=" | "<="

addingOperator = "+" | "-"

multiplyingOperator = "*" | "/" | "%"

integer = digit { digit }

double = integer "." integer

identifier = [ "_" ] letter { "_" | letter | digit }

string = """ { any printable character } """

character = "'" any printable character "'"
```

Syntax Error Messages

The C++ compiler can generate the following syntax error messages:

```
{ expected.
} expected.
; expected.
( expected.
) expected.
] expected.
= expected.
>> expected.
<< expected.
void expected.
main expected.
Identifier expected.
Illegal beginning of statement.
Letter not expected.
Unrecognized symbol.
Constant identifier not appropriate here.
Function identifier not appropriate here.
Variable identifier not appropriate here.
<identifier name> not declared.
<identifier name> already declared.
Whole array not allowed here.
Function identifier expected.
Must be void function here.
No void function here.
Integer, double, or character expected.
Incompatible data types.
Number of actual parameters must match number of formal parameters.
Right paren expected.
Identifier or number expected.
Single quote mark expected.
Character must not go to next line.
String must not go to next line.
String must not exceed <maximum number of chracacters>.
Array size must be greater than zero and less than 101.
Digit expected.
Cannot have text and graphics at the same time.
No main function defined.
Return type of main function must be void.
Output type must be string or subrange.
Numeric operand expected.
```

```
Type must be array.
Index must be integer.
Operand must be a subrange type.
Type of input datum must be int, char, or double.
int operand expected.
Type of array index must be int.
```

Run-Time Error Messages

The run-time system can generate the following error messages:

```
Integer overflow.
Divide by zero.
Stack overflow.
Value out of range.
Uninitialized variable reference.
```

Additional Notes

1. C++ is case sensitive. Thus, **main** is a reserved word, but **Main** is an identifier.
2. The primitive data types are **int**, **double**, and **char**.
3. The structured data type is `array`. The base type of an array can be **int**, **double**, or **char**.
4. Function definitions must appear above the main function definition. They may not be nested within other function definitions.
5. Variable declarations must appear within a block. They must appear after any constant definitions and before any statements (this is unlike "standard" C++, in which they can appear anywhere).
6. Binary operations (**+**, **-**, etc.) on an **int** and a **double** produce a **double** as a result.
7. An **int** value may be assigned to a **double** variable, input into a **double** variable, or passed as an actual parameter in the place of a **double** formal parameter. In these cases, the **int** value is promoted to a **double** value.
8. When a **double** value is assigned to an **int** variable or passed as an actual parameter in the place of an **int** formal parameter, the **double** value is first truncated to an **int** value.
9. When a **char** value is assigned or passed as a parameter to an **int** variable, the character's ASCII value is used.
10. When an **int** value is assigned to a **char** variable, the **int** value is subsequently treated as the character's ASCII value.

Worksheet
Lab Experience 12
C++ Programming—Input, Output, and Control Structures

Name: _____

Course: _____

Exercise 12.2. Dealing with syntax errors

Exercise 12.3. Labeling output

Exercise 12.6. Converting degrees Fahrenheit to degrees centigrade

Exercise 12.8. The `if...else` statement

Exercise 12.9. A three-way decision

Exercise 12.10. The `while` statement

Exercise 12.11. Accumulating a sum

Exercise 12.12. Accumulating a sum of a series of input values

Exercise 12.13. Accumulating a sum of absolute values

Lab Experience 13

C++ Programming—Functions and Arrays

Objectives

- Learn to design and use C++ *functions*; a function is an important *abstraction* mechanism that captures a frequently used pattern of instructions in a single named entity
- Learn to use *parameters* with functions; parameters provide a mechanism for passing data to a function so the function can perform different instances of a general task
- Learn about the *array* data structure; arrays are a useful abstraction mechanism for representing lists of data
- See how these features of C++ provide the problem solving tools needed to implement algorithms such as the searching, data cleanup, and sorting algorithms of Chapters 2 and 3

Exercise 13.1. Functions as abstraction mechanisms

Suppose you want to skip two lines between some outputs. You could accomplish that in a C++ program by means of two successive output statements. If you wanted to skip five lines, you could type in five successive output statements. Suppose that you wanted to skip the same number of lines at several places in your program. If it were just two lines at a time, you probably would not object to typing the two output statements on several occasions. However, it would definitely be irritating if you had to type five of them each time. It turns out that there is a way of removing this irritation in a C++ program. The language provides a way of packaging a frequently used sequence of statements as a single, abstract unit and giving it a name, say, **skipFiveLines**. Then, wherever you want to skip five lines in this program, you just use this new name, **skipFiveLines**, as easily as you use a single output statement. This abstraction is called a *function*.

To see how a function is defined and used, open the file **Example6.cpp** from the **File** menu. There you will see a function definition and a use of the function in the program. Compile and run the program to observe the result. Then modify the function so that it skips seven lines rather than five. Test it again.

Exercise 13.2. Generalizing functions with parameters

In general, one might skip any number of lines in an output sequence by typing just that number of output statements in a program. This can be expressed as a *general* problem: perform n output statements, where $n > 0$. We would like a general solution to this problem. However, every time we want our function from the

133

previous exercise to solve this problem for a new case of *n*, we must rewrite the function itself. Again, there is a way of providing one function in C++ to solve a problem of this kind. We can add a *parameter* to the definition of the function. The parameter, call it **n**, is a number that will specify how many output statements to execute. We can then write the function as a loop from **n** down to one, and we will have a general solution to the problem of skipping *n* lines!

To see how a parameter is defined and used, open the file **Example7.cpp** from the **File** menu. You will see a function called **skipLines**, with a single *formal parameter*, **n**. When the function is called in a given spot in the program, the programmer can specify how many lines to skip by passing an *actual parameter*, an integer value, to the function. Compile and run the program to verify that it behaves as expected. Now return to the program and change the actual parameters so that it produces different results.

Exercise 13.3. Functions that return a value

The previous examples of functions had a void return type. They were run just to perform a task. Functions can also return a single value. The type of the value returned (**int**, **double**, or **char**) is specified at the beginning of the function heading. When the function is ready to return a value to its caller, the function executes a return statement anywhere in its set of statements. The caller can then use this value in any expression.

To see how a function can return a value, open the file **Example8.cpp** from the **File** menu. You will see a function called **square**, which expects a double as its parameter, and returns a double representing the square of the parameter. Run the program with several inputs. Then add a new function called **cube** that returns the cube of its parameter. Display the cube of the input value along with its square in the output.

Exercise 13.4. Input and output parameters

In the previous exercise, you observed a function whose parameter is passed to it for its use. The function also returns a single value. The function has no need to change the value passed to it, nor does the user of the function wish that value to be changed. Therefore, we can say that we pass the value to the function as an *input parameter*. However, there are many cases where we might want the function to do some work on some data passed to it, and return more than one result. We might have these data returned to us as *output parameters*. To see how this might work, open the file **Example9.cpp** from the **File** menu. You will see a function that takes two **int** variables and exchanges their values. Note that the actual parameters must in every case be variables (why must this be so?). Compile and run the program with different test data.

Now return to the editor and delete the **&** symbols from the function heading. Compile and test the program again. Explain the results.

Exercise 13.5. The greatest common divisor

Design, implement, and test a C++ function that expects two **int** parameters and returns their greatest common divisor. Be sure to write a pseudocode algorithm first; and be sure to test the program with different pairs of numbers.

Exercise 13.6. Arrays

Recall the algorithms for searching through and sorting lists of data in Chapters 2 and 3 of the text. We can represent a list of numbers conveniently as a data structure called an *array* in C++. An array is just a collection of data values of the same type, where each value is accessible by means of a number called an *index*. For example, if we want to look up the value at the first position in an array **a**, we use the notation **a[0]** in C++. The last value in an array of size *n* would be **a[n - 1]**. We can also store a value in an array at the *i*th position by assigning the value to **a[i - 1]**. To see how arrays are defined as data structures and then manipulated, open the file **Example10.cpp** from the **File** menu. You will see a constant, **MAX**, that specifies the size or upper bound of the array. Next, you will see an array variable declaration. Finally, you will see two loops: one that gets values from the user and inserts them into the array, and the other that looks the values up in the array to display them. Compile and run the program with some test data.

Exercise 13.7. Changing the size of an array

Modify the previous program so that the array can contain five numbers (*Hint*: the constant **MAX** defines the size of the array). Test the program until it behaves as expected.

Exercise 13.8. Functions for arrays

Input and output of the contents of an array are such frequently used operations that they ought to be packaged as functions. Define two functions that do just that. They should be *general*; that is, they should work for *any* array of integers. The heading of the array output function should have the form

```
void <function name> (<element type> <array formal parameter name>[ ],
  int length)
```

where the parameter **length** represents the number of data elements in the array. The heading of the array input function should have the form

```
void <function name> (<element type> <array formal parameter name>[ ],
  int &length)
```

where the parameter **length** represents the size of the array before the data are input, and the number of data values actually entered after input.

Test your functions until they behave as expected.

Exercise 13.9. Search for a value

Define a function that searches an array for a value. It should take the target value and the array as input parameters. If the value is found, the function returns its index position; otherwise, the function returns −1. You can use the algorithm from Chapter 2 if you like. Test your function by passing values into it, asking the user for a target value, running a search, and displaying the appropriate message about the outcome of the search.

Exercise 13.10. Sorting an array

Pick your favorite data cleanup or sorting algorithm from Chapter 3 and implement it as a C++ function. Test your function using a method like the one described in the previous exercise.

Worksheet
Lab Experience 13
C++ Programming—Functions and Arrays

Name: _____

Course: _____

Exercise 13.1. Functions as abstraction mechanisms

Exercise 13.2. Generalizing functions with parameters

Exercise 13.3. Functions that return a value

Exercise 13.4. Input and output parameters

Exercise 13.5. The greatest common divisor

Exercise 13.8. Functions for arrays

Exercise 13.9. Search for a value

Exercise 13.10. Sorting an array

Lab Experience 14

C++ Programming—Graphics

Objectives

In the previous two lab experiences, you learned the features of a large subset of C++. One major drawback of this subset is that programs can interact with users only by displaying text on a terminal screen and taking text as input from the keyboard. More sophisticated programs support the display of graphical images and allow the user to signal inputs by aiming and clicking a mouse at certain spots on the screen. In the next lab experience, you will learn to use a set of graphics functions that allow you to display images and interact with a mouse.

Background

As discussed in Chapter 8 of the text, modern computers represent all output graphically, in a two-dimensional bitmap. Each pixel in this bitmap is located by specifying a point in a window's coordinate system. The origin of this coordinate system (0, 0) lies in the upper-left corner of the window. The x and y coordinates increase as we move to the left and to the bottom of the window, respectively. We assume a black and white color system.

The following table lists the graphics functions provided with our C++.

Function	What it does
`void clearscreen(int color)`	If color <= 0, sets the background color to white; otherwise, sets the background color to black.
`void setcolor(int color)`	If color <= 0, sets the pen color to white; otherwise, sets the pen color to black.
`int getmaxx()`	Returns the maximum x coordinate in the window.
`int getmaxy()`	Returns the maximum x coordinate in the window.
`void lineto(int x, int y)`	Draws a line from the current pen position to the specified coordinates.
`void moveto(int x, int y)`	Positions the pen at the specified coordinates.

Function	What it does
`void circle(int x, int y, int radius)`	Draws a circle with the specified center point coordinates and radius.
`void rectangle(int x1, int y1, int x2, int y2)`	Draws a rectangle with the specified corner points.
`void getmouse(int &x, int &y)`	Returns the coordinates of the last mouse click.
`void writedraw(string s, int x, int y)`	Draws the string s. The point (x, y) is at the baseline of the first character in the string.
`void writedraw(int i, int x, int y)`	Draws the integer i. The point (x, y) is at the baseline of the first digit in the integer.

Exercise 14.1. Put on a happy face

Open the file **Graphic1.cpp** from the C++ compiler's **File** menu. This program draws a simple face. The face consists of a large circle positioned at the center of the window and two smaller circles representing the eyes. Note how the functions **getmaxx** and **getmaxy** are used to determine the center and radius of the circle. Compile and run the program.

Now return to the editor and modify the program so that the face has nose and a mouth. A simple horizontal line will do for the mouth, although you should be able to add other lines that make the mouth curl up in a smile.

Exercise 14.2. Draw and erase a picture interactively

The file **Graphic2.cpp** contains a program that allows the user to draw a rectangle by clicking the mouse at the desired corners. The program displays messages to prompt the user for each mouse click. Compile and test the program by drawing several different rectangles.

Now modify the program as follows. After the program draws the rectangle, prompt the user to click the mouse once more to erase the rectangle. After the user clicks the mouse, set the pen color to white and draw the rectangle again. This will have the effect of erasing the original drawing.

Exercise 14.3. Inverse video

Modify the program in **Graphic2.cpp** so that it draws a white rectangle on a black background. You do this by inserting the following two lines of code at the beginning of the program:

```
clearscreen(1);
setcolor(0);
```

Compile and test the program to make sure that it performs just as it did in Exercise 14.2, but in inverse video.

Exercise 14.4. Draw the coordinates

Open the file **Graphic3.cpp** from the **File** menu. This program displays the coordinates of the first five mouse clicks. Compile and run the program.

Now modify the program so that it displays the coordinates of any number of mouse clicks, until the user clicks at the bottom edge of the window.

Exercise 14.5. Animation

One way to animate an image is to repeatedly draw it, erase it, adjust its coordinates, and redraw it. The file **Graphic4.cpp** contains a program that moves a circle across the middle of the window. Compile and run this program.

Now modify the program so that it "bounces" the circle off the right edge of the window and returns it to the left edge.

Exercise 14.6. Defining a graphics function

The file **Graphic5.cpp** contains a function, **drawFace**, to draw the face displayed in the first program of this lab. The program prompts the user to click the mouse three times. When the user clicks the mouse, the program passes the coordinates as parameters to the function, which draws the circle at these coordinates. Compile and run the program.

Now modify the program by defining a new function, **drawHouse**, to draw a house. A simple triangle atop a rectangle will do. The function should take as parameters the x and y coordinates of the peak of the house's roof. After the user clicks the mouse, the program should draw the face as before, and also draw the house 50 points to the right of the face.

Exercise 14.7. A fractal image

A fractal is a mathematical object that exhibits a repetitive pattern when visualized. A c-curve is a simple kind of fractal that is constructed as follows:

1. A level 0 c-curve is a line segment.
2. A level 1 c-curve consists of a line segment divided in two and bent at right angles. Each of these shorter line segments is actually a level 0 c-curve.
3. A level n c-curve consists of two level $n-1$ c-curves constructed in this way.

This definition of the c-curve is called a *recursive definition*. A recursive definition consists of one or more simple cases (in this example, a level 0 c-curve is a line segment) and one or more recursive cases (a level n c-curve consists of two level $n-1$ c-curves). A recursive definition in part defines a thing in terms of itself.

Recursive definitions can be translated to recursive algorithms and then to recursive functions in a programming language. You saw an example of a recursive algorithm for quick sort in Lab Experience 6. Recursive functions have:

1. a simple case, in which a task is performed directly, and
2. a recursive case, in which a task is performed by calling the same function again.

The file **Graphic6.cpp** contains a recursive function, **cCurve**, for drawing c-curves. When the level of the c-curve becomes zero, the function draws a simple line segment and quits. Otherwise, the function draws two c-curves of level $n-1$. Compile and run this program. It should draw a level 0 c-curve. Now test the program with levels 1, 2, 4, 8, and 12 (you will have to return to the editor after each test to modify the parameter passed as the level).

How many calls of the **cCurve** function are made during the drawing of a level 12 c-curve?

Worksheet
Lab Experience 14
C++ Programming—Graphics

Name: _____

Course: _____

Exercise 14.1. Put on a happy face

Exercise 14.2. Draw and erase a picture interactively

Exercise 14.4. Draw the coordinates

Exercise 14.5. Animation

Exercise 14.6. Defining a graphics function

Exercise 14.7. A fractal image

Lab Experience 15

HTML and FTP Downloading

Objectives

- Learn some of the most basic features of HTML (HyperText Markup Language), the underlying language for creating Web pages
- Create a simple Web page
- Use a Web browser to perform simple file transfers with FTP (File Transfer Protocol), the basic protocol for Internet file transfers

Background

You have read about the history of the Web, the algorithms and protocols that make such networking endeavors possible, and some of the social implications of the Web. In this lab session, you will practice using some of the most basic features of HTML to make your own Web pages. This opens the door for you to become a contributor to the Web enterprise rather than simply a user of the Web. You will also learn how to use your Web browser to perform simple file transfers from FTP servers. Creating Web documents with HTML is somewhat analogous to writing programs in assembly language. Today there are many Web editors available to simplify the process of writing Web pages. In fact, the Web browsers and most word processors include facilities for creating Web pages. You might think of Web editors as the high level languages of Web production. Just as programs written in high level languages such as C++, LISP, or PROLOG must be translated to machine or assembly language before they can be executed, documents written using Web editors are converted to HTML before they are viewed as Web pages. In this lab you will work directly with HTML. Just as learning a little about assembly language helps you understand what is going on inside the computer and helps you understand the features of a high level language, learning the basics of HTML is important for understanding the underlying process of Web page formatting and design. Another practical reason for learning about HTML is that you will often see some attractive feature that a Web author has used on a page. Using your browser you will be able to look at the source of the page. However, the source will be the HTML file for the page. This is true even if a fancy Web editor was used to create the document. So, to learn by example requires knowing about HTML. Once you have practiced the basic features of HTML, you may well want to learn to use a Web editor. Most word processors and Web browsers include tutorials that teach you how to use the special Web editing features that they provide. The discussion that follows is based somewhat on *A Beginner's Guide to HTML* which was developed at the National Center for Supercomputer Applications and is present on many World Wide Web servers.

151

Recall from the text that much of the formatting of HTML is achieved with pairs of **tags** that enclose the text to which the formatting action applies. The beginning tag of a pair is usually of the form <action-symbol>, and the ending tag of the pair is of the form </action-symbol>. Here the action symbol is a special code indicating the manipulation that should be applied to the text enclosed between the pair of tags. For example, the symbol B indicates boldface. Thus <B> Lab Manual </B> in an HTML file causes the text "Lab Manual" to be displayed in boldface on the Web page. Keep in mind that tag pairs can be nested within each other just as parentheses pairs can be nested in arithmetic expressions. For example, the HTML expression

<B> Just bold <I> Both bold and italic </I> Just bold </B> Plain

displays on the page as

Just bold *Both bold and italic* Just bold Plain

because the italic tag pair is included within the bold tag pair. Here is a list of basic tags together with their uses. Unless mentioned specifically, these occur in pairs. There are many books and online tutorials on HTML. There you will find more tags and HTML features.

HTML This tag indicates that the enclosed material is written in HTML. Therefore your entire HTML document should begin with <HTML> and end with </HTML>.

HEAD There are two major sections of an HTML document—the head and the body. This tag and its partner mark the beginning and end of the head section. This section does not contain material that will actually appear on the page itself. Primarily, it contains the title of the document.

TITLE This tag and its partner enclose the title of the page. This is placed within the head section of the document. The title does not appear on the page itself but does appear in the title bar of the window. Another important use of the title is that it appears in the bookmark list if the page has been saved by anyone as a bookmark.

BODY This pair of tags marks the beginning and end of the body section of the document. This section includes all of the text of the page together with the HTML tags for formatting the page and linking the page to other pages on the Web. These four tags are actually enough to create a simple Web page. As mentioned in the text, a minimal HTML document would look like this:

```
<HTML>
<HEAD>
<TITLE> Title of your choice </TITLE>
</HEAD>
<BODY>
        Text of your choice
</BODY>
</HTML>
```

If you created such a file with a text editor and named the file with a filename ending in .html, you should be able to open the file as a Web page using your Web browser.

H1   There are six levels of headings in HTML. These are numbered H1 through H6, with H1 being the largest and boldest. These are used to provide headings for divisions of your page. For example, you might use H1 for the main heading of your page and use H2 for section headings within the page. Some browsers may not distinguish six distinct levels.

P   This tag is used to mark the beginning of a new paragraph. HTML ignores line breaks and extra spaces between words in the text. Therefore the P tag is important to cause line separation between paragraphs. Optionally, you can use the P tag to specify how the paragraph should be aligned. For example, you can use <P ALIGN=CENTER> to center the paragraph on the page.

UL   HTML supports several types of lists such as unnumbered lists, numbered or ordered lists, and definition lists. This tag indicates an unnumbered, bulleted list.

OL   This tag is used for an ordered or numbered list. Note that lists can be nested with different list types being nested within each other.

LI   This tag indicates the beginning of a list item within a list. No closing tag is needed. You should now study carefully the HTML file shown in Figure 15.1. Be sure that you understand how the nested lists produce the page shown in Figure 15.2. Here we have two ordered lists nested as list items within the unnumbered list.

```
<HTML>
<HEAD>
<TITLE> Programming Languages </TITLE>
</HEAD>
<BODY>
<H1> Programming Languages in CS322 </H1>
<H2> An Outline of Languages </H2>
<UL>
<LI> Procedural Languages
<OL>
<LI> FORTRAN
<LI> COBOL
<LI> Pascal
<LI> C
<LI> Ada
</OL>
<LI> Object Oriented Languages
<OL>
<LI> C++
<LI> Java
<LI> Smalltalk
</OL>
</UL>
</BODY>
</HTML>
```

Figure 15.1 An HTML file with nested lists

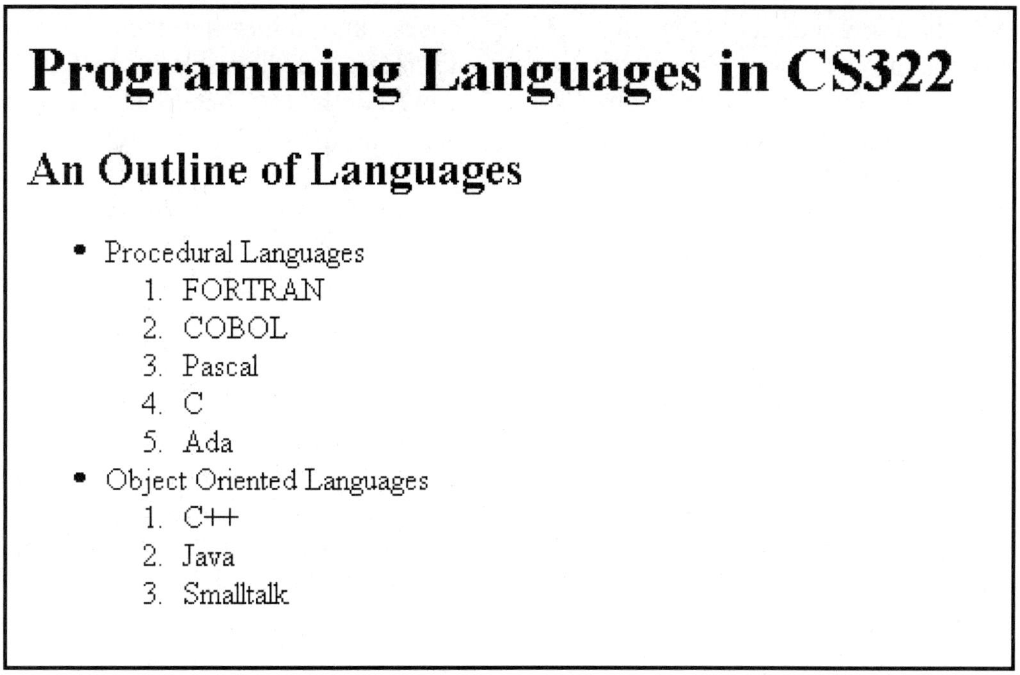

Programming Languages in CS322

An Outline of Languages

- Procedural Languages
    1. FORTRAN
    2. COBOL
    3. Pascal
    4. C
    5. Ada
- Object Oriented Languages
    1. C++
    2. Java
    3. Smalltalk

Figure 15.2 The Web page produced from HTML code of Figure 15.1

BR   This tag causes a line break to occur. While the P tag causes a blank line to appear between the paragraphs, the BR tag simply causes the following text to appear on the next line. Because regular line breaks in the text are ignored, this is an important feature for those situations where you want to make sure that the following text begins on a new line. The BR tag is used alone without an end tag.

HR   This horizontal rule tag also occurs without an end tag and causes a neat horizontal line to occur. This is often used to separate sections of a page.

B   As mentioned earlier, this tag pair is used to have text appear in boldface.

I   Again, this is used for putting text in italics.

A   The anchor tag pair is used to create links—probably the most important feature in HTML. This topic is complicated because of the wide variety of types of objects that we might wish to access via links. The possibilities include other pages within the same directory as the current page, other pages on the same Web server but in another directory, specific locations within the current page or other pages, pages stored on other World Wide Web servers, images (sound, video, etc.) at any of these locations, files to be downloaded from FTP servers which allow public access for such purposes, and telnet services allowing the use of computational resources on another computer. Here we discuss how to link to pages in the same directory, to pages on other servers using URLs, to other locations within the current page, and to objects on public Web servers. Later in this section, we discuss linking to images and to public FTP servers.

In addition to the code A, the beginning tag contains the target address for the link. The form for this tag is <A HREF="target-address">. If we are linking to another file in the same directory, then the target address is simply the filename. Note that filenames of HTML files should always end in .html. To link to files in other directories, you must use the pathname to the file. To link to pages on other servers, you simply use the URL as the target address in the tag. As you know, URLs to Web pages begin with *http*. This indicates that we are linking to a file on a World Wide Web server. There are specifications other than *http* that allow linking to objects other than Web pages. For example, *FTP* indicates that we are linking to an FTP server that allows public access, and *telnet* indicates a link to a server providing computational services. We shall discuss the *FTP* option more fully a little later in this section.

The end tag is simply </A> as you would expect. Between the two tags is the text that should appear highlighted and which is clicked to execute the link. For example, if you wanted a link from your page to a popular page for learning about the weather, you could put in the HTML expression

<A HREF= http://www.weatherhub.com/> Web Exercises </A>

With long documents it is often convenient to have links to various sections within the document. For example, if the document is divided into chapters, you might like to have a table of contents at the beginning with links to the various chapters. To do this requires not only the links to go to the various chapters, but also a new type of anchor naming locations within the document to which we can link. The form for this new type of anchor is

<A NAME="location-name"> Location-title </A>.

Here the location-name is a name that will be used in the anchors that link to this spot, and the location title will appear at the top of the screen when such a link is activated. For example, if we wish to allow links to Chapter 2 on tree searching algorithms, we could provide a name anchor of the form

<A NAME="Ch2"> Chapter 2 - Tree Searching Algorithms </A>.

Since we want the chapter title to serve as a heading, we would probably include the entire anchor within a heading tag pair, say like

<H2> <A NAME="Ch2"> Chapter 2 - Tree Searching Algorithms </A> </H2>.

Now to provide a link to such a named location, the anchor is of the form

<A HREF="#location-name"> Link-text </A>

where location-name is the named location to which we are linking, and Link-text is the text for the highlighted link used to activate the transfer. So, in the table of contents we might have links of the form

<A HREF="#Ch2"> Chapter 2 </A>

or

<A HREF="#Ch2"> Tree Scarching Algorithms </A>

or

<A HREF="#Ch2"> Chapter 2 - Tree Searching Algorithms </A>,

etc.

IMG   This tag occurs without a partner and is used for displaying images on a page. As discussed in the text, images are stored as special files with information such as color for each pixel of the image. There are several formats that are widely used for storing such images. Two of the most common formats are GIF and JPEG, and files in these formats are named with endings *.gif* and *.jpeg*, respectively. The Web browsers are usually capable of displaying images that are stored in these formats. The form of the anchor is

<IMG SRC=image-location>

where the image-location is the filename of the image on the computer where the page is stored or the URL for the image file on another computer. For example, if you have a picture of yourself stored in the file *me.gif*, then you can have it displayed on your page using the anchor

<IMG SRC=me.gif>.

The IMG tag also allows an optional ALIGN clause following the filename. This has to do with how the image is aligned with the text. For example,

<IMG SRC=me.gif ALIGN=CENTER>

will place the image at the left with one line of text to the right of the image and centered vertically with the picture. You can also use TOP rather than CENTER. This puts one line to the right and at the top of the picture. The default is to have the one line of text to the right of the bottom line of the picture. To have a picture appear by itself without text to the right, put the IMG tag in a paragraph by itself. You can then use ALIGN with the paragraph tag to justify the image as you please. You can also link to an image using an anchor. For example, if you have a large picture of yourself that you do not want to appear on your page, you might use a link such as the following

<A HREF="me.gif"> A picture of me </A>.

If someone clicks on the words "A picture of me", the browser should display your picture.

To create an HTML file, you can use any text editor or word processor. Once you have created an HTML file on your local computer, you can view the resulting page with your Web browser. To do this, select the **Open** option under the **File** menu and then select the HTML file that you have created. If you need to make changes, you can edit the file in another window, save the file, and then use the **Reload** button of the browser to view the new version of your page. In order to have your page available for other users of the Web, your HTML file must be stored on a Web server. Most colleges and universities have Web servers, but you will need to check with the local experts for the details for doing this. Many businesses have their own Web servers or else pay for space on Web servers of companies who specialize in providing Internet services for their customers.

As with Web servers, many institutions provide FTP servers. These servers usually have many directories, each storing many related files. These files may be textual documents, graphics, or pieces of special purpose software that can be transferred from the server to the user's local computer—this is called *downloading*. In order to download a file from an FTP server, you must be able to log onto the server machine. While many servers restrict access to authorized users, others allow *anonymous* logins. In this case the user name "anonymous" with any password—often your e-mail address is requested as a password—yields access to the server. While there are many excellent programs specifically for managing FTP transfers, the standard Web browsers can also be used for downloading files from FTP servers that allow anonymous logins. To use your browser for this purpose, simply use the *FTP* prefix in the URL rather than the *http* prefix. This type of URL can be used in the location field or in the anchor of a link. Exactly what the browser does with the file depends on the type of file accessed. If it is reasonable, the browser will display the text or image; otherwise, it may simply ask if you would like to save the file on your computer (download). In the former case, you can download the file by selecting the **Save** option under the **File** menu.

Exercise 15.1. Viewing HTML code

In this exercise, you will view some HTML code. Start up your browser and go to the page http://www.wlu.edu/~lambertk/invitation/example.html. To view the HTML code for this page, choose **Source** (Internet Explorer) or **Page Source** (Netscape Navigator) under the **View** menu. This should display the HTML source in another window. By comparing the source together with the page displayed, answer the following questions on the Worksheet page for this lab:

1. Give the title of the page.
2. Describe one use of lists on the page.
3. Describe one use of a link on the page.
4. Describe one tag used on the page that was not described in our discussion in the Background section of this lab.

Exercise 15.2. Making your own page

For this exercise you will use a text editor or word processor to create an HTML file containing information about yourself. Your page should be divided into the following sections:

1. Brief family history.
2. Brief educational history. Include a list of schools you have attended.
3. Current academic situation. Include information about your major, your current school (with a link to school's home page), and a list of courses you are taking.
4. Non-academic interests. Include information about hobbies, favorite musical groups, etc.

You should have a table of contents at the beginning with links to the various sections. Separate the sections with horizontal lines. To view your page, run your Web browser, select the **Open** option under the **File** menu, and then select the HTML file that you have created. When you have the page the way you want it, click on the **Print** button of the browser to print a copy of the page to turn in. To get a copy of the HTML code to turn in, use the **Print** option under the **File** menu of your text editor or word processor.

Exercise 15.3. Downloading with the browser

In this exercise, you will simply download a text file from an FTP server. To do this, type the URL

http://www.wlu.edu/~lambertk/invitation/example.txt

into the location field of your browser. The browser will probably display the short text file. You should then select the **Save As** option under the **File** menu to bring the file from the server to your computer.

Worksheet
Lab Experience 15
HTML and FTP Downloading

Name: _____

Course: _____

Exercise 15.1. Viewing HTML code

Page title:

Use of lists:

Use of a link:

New use of a tag:

Lab Experience 16

LISP Programming

Objectives

- Obtain an introduction to programming in LISP
- See how the LISP environment and language provide another layer of virtual machine between the programmer and the computer
- See how LISP programmers can solve problems at a higher level of abstraction than C++ programmers

Background

In Chapter 8 of the text, you were introduced to some of the features of a high-level programming language, C++. You learned that C++ supports the direct coding of the major control structures of pseudo-code algorithms: sequencing, selection, and iteration. C++ also supports the abstraction mechanisms of functions and arrays. In each case, the C++ language allows programmers to express their solutions in terms of standard control and data abstractions, without worrying about how these are implemented on a real machine.

Nevertheless, there are several respects in which the use of C++ does not insulate programmers from machine details as much as they might like. In each of these areas, LISP provides features that sharpen the abstraction barrier between the programmer and the machine.

Memory management

C++ relieves the programmer of many, but not all, of the details of moving data around in memory. For example, evaluating the expression $2 + x$ in assembly language requires a **load** and a **store** operation as well as an **add** operation. The C++ expression specifies just the addition, with no (apparent) data movement. However, the values of expressions in C++ programs are usually stored in variables with the assignment statement, for example, $y = 2 + x$. Indeed, a very large percentage of statements in C++ programs are assignment statements, whose sole purpose is to move data from one place in memory to another. Thus, much of the work of a C++ programmer still involves managing memory.

LISP provides an assignment statement, but its use is not necessary, and good LISP programming practice minimizes it. Good LISP programs consist of combinations of expressions. Data movement occurs only in the underlying virtual machine, where it is completely invisible to the programmer.

Control abstraction

One reason that the assignment statement is so prevalent in C++ programs is that it is used to control iteration. For example, just before a **while** statement, the programmer must initialize a control variable with an assignment statement. Then one must increment or decrement the control variable within the loop, in either case with an assignment statement.

LISP also provides a loop statement, but again, its use is not necessary, and good LISP programming practice minimizes it. Iteration in good LISP programs is implemented by *recursive functions*.

Procedural abstraction

C++ allows programmers to capture common patterns of instructions in functions, whose parameters specialize the patterns for different data. However, C++ does not support very well the *combination* of these patterns into more general or higher-order patterns. For example, one might want to write a function that applies another function to each item in a list of data and returns a list of the results. Or one might want to write a function that takes two other functions as parameters and returns a composite function as the result. The first problem is quite difficult to solve in C++; the second problem is impossible to solve in C++.

LISP functions generalize C++ functions. LISP functions treat any LISP objects—numbers, lists, and even other functions—as *first class data*. That is, any LISP object, including a function, can be passed as a parameter to a LISP function and returned as its value. This feature makes the creation of higher-order functions a virtual requirement of good LISP programming practice.

Data abstraction

C++ provides several built-in data structures, such as arrays. C++ also supports the combination of built-in data structures to form new data structures. However, the built-in data structures are very limited. If programmers wish to use a data structure whose size can grow or shrink at run-time and whose component elements can be of different types, they must write all of the primitive operations on this structure themselves.

The primary built-in data structure in LISP is the list. LISP provides many useful operators for adding data of any type to lists, accessing data in lists, and performing high-order tasks, such as mapping, on lists. In addition, since LISP lists look exactly like LISP expressions or programs, the programmer can explicitly "store" a program in a data structure and execute it on demand.

Category of virtual machine

The built-in data, operators, and control structures of C++ provide the programmer with a model of a high-level von Neumann machine, but a von Neumann machine nonetheless. The primary characteristics of this model are sequential execution of instructions, branching to other areas of program memory, and movement of data within memory.

LISP provides the programmer with a very different model of a virtual machine. This model, whose primary characteristic is the combination of expressions and recursive functions, is called the *recursive lambda calculus*. Not only does this model yield more natural solutions to a wide range of problems in different domains, but the solutions themselves are much more susceptible to rigorous mathematical analysis for correctness and efficiency. In addition to the standard LISP virtual machine, LISP provides access to other virtual machines in two directions. First, a small set of primitives such as an assignment statement serve as "hooks" to the underlying von Neumann machine. Second, LISP allows the programmer to construct interpreters for "metalanguages" that represent other models of virtual machines that you studied Chapter 8 of the text, such as automated theorem-proving and objects with message-passing.

Programming environment

C++ is definitely a higher-level language than assembly language. However, C++ programmers go through much the same process as assembly language programmers to construct, translate, and test their programs. They all must deal with a *batch processing* system; they use a text editor, then a compiler, and finally a run-time system to finish a program.

LISP programs are constructed and run in the same, interactive environment. This environment, known as an *interpreter*, gives programmers instant feedback on the effectiveness of their solutions, and allows them to develop large systems incrementally.

The following exercises will introduce you to the features of LISP enumerated above. You should begin by running your local LISP interpreter. The examples shown here are written in a dialect of LISP called Scheme. You may have to change some syntax if you are using a more traditional LISP. A free Scheme interpreter can be downloaded from **www.plt-scheme.org/software.html**.

Exercise 16.1. Composing expressions

The simplest expressions in LISP are called *atoms*. Type each of the following atoms at the interpreter's prompt, and note the values returned:

```
3
3.14
```

```
"Hi there"

#\a
+

sqrt
```

Now type each of the following *compound expressions* at the interpreter's prompt, and note the values returned (be sure to place spaces between the numbers and operators):

```
(+ 3 2)

(* 5 (+ 3 2))

(* 3.14 (* 3 3))

(sqrt (- 4 2))
```

Exercise 16.2. Defining and using functions

LISP lets us define functions quite easily. They can then be used just like the built-in functions **+** and **abs** that you saw in the first exercise. Define a function **square** by typing the following expression at the interpreter's prompt:

```
(define (square x)
  (* x x))
```

Then test it by typing these expressions at the prompt:

```
(square 3)

(+ (square 3) (square 4))

(square (square 3))
```

Exercise 16.3. Defining and using predicates or Boolean expressions

A *predicate* is a function that tests a value for a property, returns true if the value satisfies that property, and false otherwise. Type the following atoms, representing true and false, at the interpreter's prompt:

```
#t

#f
```

Now type the following expressions and note the values returned:

```
(= 2 3)

(= 2 2)

(zero? 0)

(odd? 1)

(atom? "Hi there")

(number? "Hi there")

(not (zero? 1))

(and (>= 2 1) (<= 2 10))
```

Suppose we wanted a new predicate, **in-range?**, that takes three integer parameters and determines whether or not the first integer lies between the other two. Type the following definition of this predicate at the prompt:

```
(define (in-range? number low high)
  (and (>= number low) (<= number high)))
```

Now test it with several numbers to verify that it works correctly.

Exercise 16.4. Making choices with the conditional expression

LISP provides a control structure called the *conditional expression* that works like an **if** statement in C++. It tests a condition, and runs either a consequent expression or an alternative expression, depending on the truth value of the condition. The entire conditional expression then returns the value of the consequent or the alternative expression.

Type the following conditional expression at the interpreter's prompt:

```
(if (> 4 3)
  4
  3)
```

Now we'll define a function that solves a general problem, finding the maximum of two numbers, using the conditional expression:

```
(define (maximum x y)
  (if (> x y)
  x
  y))
```

Test this function with several pairs of numbers.

Exercise 16.5. Iterating with recursion

Consider the problem of computing the factorial of a number, say, 4. The factorial of 4 would be 4 * 3 * 2 * 1 = 24. In general, the factorial of any positive number, n, is n * (n - 1) * (n - 2) * . . . * 1. In C++, we could solve this problem with a **while** loop:

```
factorial = 1;
while (n > 0)
{
 factorial = factorial * n;
 n = n - 1;
}
```

However, there is a much simpler *recursive* definition of the factorial of a number. It consists of two cases:
```
n! = 1, when n = 0.
n! = n * (n - 1)!, when n > 0.
```

These two cases translate directly to a LISP function that uses a conditional expression and a *recursive call*, rather than a loop:
```
(define (factorial n)
(if (zero? n)
1
(* n (factorial (- n 1))))))
```

Test this function with several numbers. If your interpreter has a trace feature, turn it on with **(trace factorial)** and run the function again with several numbers.

The greatest common divisor of two integers is the largest integer by which both are evenly divisible. You saw an iterative version of Euclid's method for computing this value in Chapter 8, Exercise 1. The method is defined recursively as follows:

```
gcd(a, b) = a, when b = 0.
gcd(a, b) = gcd(b, remainder of dividing a by b), when b > 0.
```

Using the **remainder** function, the conditional expression, and a recursive call, define and test a LISP function that computes the greatest common divisor of two integers.

Exercise 16.6. Using symbols and quotation

LISP was originally designed for processing the lists of symbols used in algebraic expressions. A *symbol* in LISP is a special kind of atom. You have seen some symbols in previous exercises, such as **abs**, **square**, and **+**. These symbols also serve as names of LISP functions: you can verify that by typing them at the interpreter's prompt to see what happens. Other symbols, such as **ken** and **tom**, may not be the names of LISP objects at all: if you type them at the prompt, you might get an error message. These symbols may mean something to us, however, and we would like the interpreter to treat them just as symbols. To do this, we prefix the symbol with a single quote mark ('). The quote mark informs the interpreter that it should return just the thing quoted; indeed, you may quote any LISP expression to achieve this effect. Type out the following quoted expressions at the prompt:

```
'ken

'tom

'abs

'(ken and tom are the authors of this manual)

'(+ 3 4)
```

Note that some of the expressions look like LISP programs that should return numbers, but they do not. Now try typing each expression without the quote mark and note the difference in the results.

Exercise 16.7. Constructing and accessing lists

The list is the basic data structure in LISP. A list looks just like a compound expression. Lists can be of arbitrary size, and they can contain any LISP data objects. For example, the list (ken and tom are the authors of this manual) contains nine symbols, while the list **(+ 3 4)** contains one symbol and two integers. The interpreter takes a compound expression to be a list if it is quoted; otherwise, it takes the expression to be the application of a function to its parameters. Thus, one way to construct a list is simply to quote it at the prompt. Another way is to use the function **list**. For example, the list (ken and tom are the authors of this manual) could be constructed by typing

```
(list 'ken 'and 'tom 'are 'the 'authors 'of 'this 'manual)
```

You should verify that this is the case now. Then try

```
(list ken and tom are the authors of this manual)
```

The most primitive list constructor is the function **cons**. To construct a list of one element, you apply **cons** to the element and the empty list, represented as a quoted pair of empty parentheses:

```
(cons 'ken '())

(cons 2 '())

(cons + '())
```

To construct a list of two or more elements, more **cons**es are required:

```
(cons 'ken (cons 'tom '()))

(cons '+ (cons 3 (cons 4 '())))
```

Once you have a list, you can access two parts: the first element in it, and a list containing the rest of the elements in the list after the first one. The function **car** returns the first element, while the function **cdr** returns the list of the remaining elements. Type the following expressions at the prompt to see this:

```
(car '(tom and ken))

(cdr '(tom and ken))

(car (cdr '(tom and ken)))

(cdr (cdr (cdr '(tom and ken))))
```

Exercise 16.8. Recursive list processing

Suppose we wanted to determine the length of a list. It turns out that **length** is a built-in function that we can already use for this purpose. For example the expression (length '(hello there)) should return 2.

Now suppose that we had to define this function ourselves. One way to do this is to define the length of a list recursively:

```
length(list) = 0, when list is empty.
length(list) = 1 +
  length(the rest of the list after the first element), otherwise.
```

All we need is a predicate to test the list to see if it's empty. The built-in predicate **null?** does this. If the list is not empty, we add one to the length of the rest of the list after the first element, by calling our function recursively with the **cdr** of the list as its parameter:

```
(define (our-length lyst)
 (if (null? lyst)
 0
 (+ 1 (our-length (cdr lyst)))))
```

Put a trace on this function if your system supports it, and run the function with lists of various lengths.

Exercise 16.9. Defining and using higher-order functions

Suppose we wanted to compute the summation of a series of integers between a lower and an upper bound. Here is a recursive definition of a summation:

```
sum(low, high) = 0, when low > high
sum(low, high) = low + sum(low + 1, high), otherwise
```

The corresponding recursive function in LISP is quite easily defined:

```
(define (sum low high)
 (if (> low high)
 0
 (+ low (sum (+ low 1) high))))
```

Run this function with several pairs of numbers and a tracer on, if possible.

Now suppose we want to take the summation of the squares of all the integers in a series. We could write another function that does just what **sum** does, but it adds the square of **low** to the sum of the rest of the series:

```
(define (sum low high)
 (if (> low high)
 0
```

```
(+ (square low) (sum (+ low 1) high))))
```

In fact, there may be numerous functions like `square` that we wish to apply during summations. Instead of writing a separate summation function for each special case, we would like to capture the general pattern of summations in one function and parameterize it for the special functions we wish to apply. All we need to do is add a parameter for the special function to our original function:

```
(define (sum low high proc)
 (if (> low high)
 0
 (+ (proc low) (sum (+ low 1) high proc))))
```

Instead of **square**, we see **proc**, which can be any function whose parameter is an integer and whose return value is also an integer. Now you can run the new version of `sum` with the **square** function you defined earlier, for example:

```
(sum 1 5 square)
```

Worksheet
Lab Experience 16
LISP Programming

Name: _____

Course: _____

Exercise 16.1. Composing expressions

Write the values:

```
(+ 3 2)

(* 5 (+ 3 2))

(* 3.14 (* 3 3))

(sqrt (- 4 2))
```

Exercise 16.2. Defining and using functions

Write the values:

```
(square 3)

(+ (square 3) (square 4))

(square (square 3))
```

Exercise 16.3. Defining and using predicates or Boolean expressions

Write the values:

```
(= 2 3)

(= 2 2)

(zero? 0)

(odd? 1)

(atom? "Hi there")

(number? "Hi there")

(not (zero? 1))

(and (>= 2 1) (<= 2 10))
```

Exercise 16.4. Making choices with the conditional expression

Write the value:

```
(if (> 4 3)
 4
 3)
```

Exercise 16.5. Iterating with recursion

Write your definition of the **gcd** function in Scheme:

Exercise 16.7. Constructing and accessing lists

Write the values:

```
(cons 'ken '())

(cons 2 '())

(cons + '())

(cons 'ken (cons 'tom '()))

(cons '+ (cons 3 (cons 4 '())))

(car '(tom and ken))

(cdr '(tom and ken))

(car (cdr '(tom and ken)))

(cdr (cdr (cdr '(tom and ken))))
```

Lab Experience 17

Programming Language Translation

Objectives

- Gain insight into the translation process for converting one virtual machine to another
- See the process by which an assembler translates assembly language into machine language
- See some of the major steps of the process a compiler would use to translate programs using a small subset of C++ into assembly language

Background

In previous lab experiences, you observed programs in three very different programming languages. You began with a language whose form maps directly to the physical structure of a real computer. You expressed instructions and data in terms of strings of 1s and 0s in this language. The computer easily understood what these strings meant, but you probably had to go through a painful process of translation to figure out what you were saying in machine language. Then you learned to use a language that still reflects the structure of the computer, but employs terms that are closer to those you would use if you were describing the instructions and data to another person. This language requires a program called an assembler to translate programs to machine language. Finally, you learned to use a language whose sentences more closely resemble those you would use in English to describe the solution of a problem. This language, C++, requires a program called a compiler to translate your sentences into machine language.

The main point of these lab exercises was not only to show you that there are different languages for expressing programs. The languages you used also represent layers of virtual machine bridging the gap between the structure of a real computer and the structure of your thoughts. It is no exaggeration to say that if this gap had not been bridged, most of the interesting and useful software that we have would not exist.

The disciplines of programming language design and translation are concerned with constructing languages and translators that help to close the conceptual gap between computers and human beings. The purpose of the present lab experience is to expose you to the translation process for converting one virtual machine into another. The following lab exercises will allow you to explore what happens when a program translates code in one language into code in another language. First, you will examine how an assembler translates an assembly language program to a machine language program. Then you will study the process by which a C++ compiler translates a C++ program to an assembly language program.

For the following exercises, select the **Assembler** from the main menu.

Exercise 17.1. Syntax analysis

Open the file **Example1.asm** from the **File** menu of the assembler. You should see the assembly language program for adding two numbers in the source pane. Select **Assemble** from the **Assembler** menu. You should see a program listing appear in the listing pane, with no syntax errors reported. Before a program can be translated, the translator must verify that there are no syntax errors in the source program. Now go back to the source pane and edit the program by changing **.begin** to **begin** (just delete the period from that line). Run the assembler again and watch what happens. Do you see where the error occurred, and was the message about it informative? Now put the period back in front of **begin** and edit the source program again, by deleting the **t** from **halt**. What kind of message do you suppose you will see this time? Why do you think that the assembler bothers to signal that there are syntax errors and to require that programs be syntactically correct before allowing the process to continue?

Exercise 17.2. Static semantic analysis

Static semantic analysis is the part of the translation process that obtains information about the meanings of identifiers (variables, constants, types, and functions) at compile time. Reload the example assembly language program, and edit it by replacing **add y** with **add a**. Assemble the program and think about the error message. Suppose that the assembler ignored errors of this sort. What do you think would happen when the computer tried to execute the instruction **add a**? Now reload the program, and insert the instruction **jump q** right after **.begin**. Assemble the program and explain the error. Insert a label for **q** before **halt** and reassemble. Then insert the label **k** before **add y** and reassemble. What are the rules governing instruction labels in assembly language, and how are they different from variable labels? Now reload the program, and change the number 4 to 32768 and reassemble. What sort of error is this, and why is it important to detect it?

Exercise 17.3. Object code

Reload the example assembly language program, assemble it, and select **View Object Code** from the **Assembler** menu. Is there a one-to-one correspondence between each assembly language instruction or datum and each machine code instruction or datum? Is there a direct mapping between the sentences of assembly language and the sentences of machine language? Verify from the table of opcodes in Lab Experience 9 that this is so. Now pick **Execute** from the **Assembler** menu. Step through the execution of the program by the machine language interpreter. Try to describe how machine language and assembly language are similar. Try to describe what is involved in translating a single assembly language instruction to a machine code instruction (picking an instruction from the example program will help).

Exercise 17.4. Symbol table

Return to the assembler from the machine language interpreter, and pick **View Symbol Table** from the **Assembler** menu. Verify that the address of each data label is correct. Why are there no instruction labels in the table? Add an instruction label to the source program, reassemble, and view the symbol table once more. Is the address of the instruction label correct? How do you suppose that the assembler uses the symbol table to detect errors in the source program?

For the following exercises, select **Language Translation** from the main menu.

Exercise 17.5. Syntax analysis

Open the program **Example1.cpp** from the **File** menu. You should see a C++ program displaying the sum of two numbers in the source pane. Pick **Compile** from the **Translator** menu. This is the only C++ program in the Examples folder that compiles correctly in this lab. The reason for this is that the subset of C++ used for this lab is much smaller than the one used in labs 12-14. In particular, the present version of C++ lacks the data types **double**, **char**, **string**, and **array**, and the operators *****, **/**, and **%**. Moreover, you cannot define functions. The reason for this is that these features do not translate to features supported by our assembly language.

Now try introducing the following syntax errors into the program, making sure that you reload the program from the file for each experiment:

a. Delete the word **main**, and compile.

b. Delete the first **{**, and compile.

c. Delete the first assignment operator (**=**), and compile.

d. Delete the addition operator (**+**), and compile.

How informative are the syntax error messages of this compiler, as compared with those generated by the assembler? Why is the compiler so fussy about C++'s syntax?

Exercise 17.6. Static semantic analysis

Change the word **sum** to the word **result** in the list of variables declared at the top of the program, and compile it. What information do the error messages provide? Why do you suppose that C++ identifiers must be declared before they are used in statements? Now change the number 4 to a large number, such as 32768.

Compile the program and explain why it is useful that the compiler catches this error before the program is translated and executed. Also explain why the compiler allows the number 32767.

Exercise 17.7. Object code

Reload and compile the example program. Select **View Object Code** from the **Translator** menu. You should see the equivalent program in assembly language in the Object Code pane (see Figure 17.1).

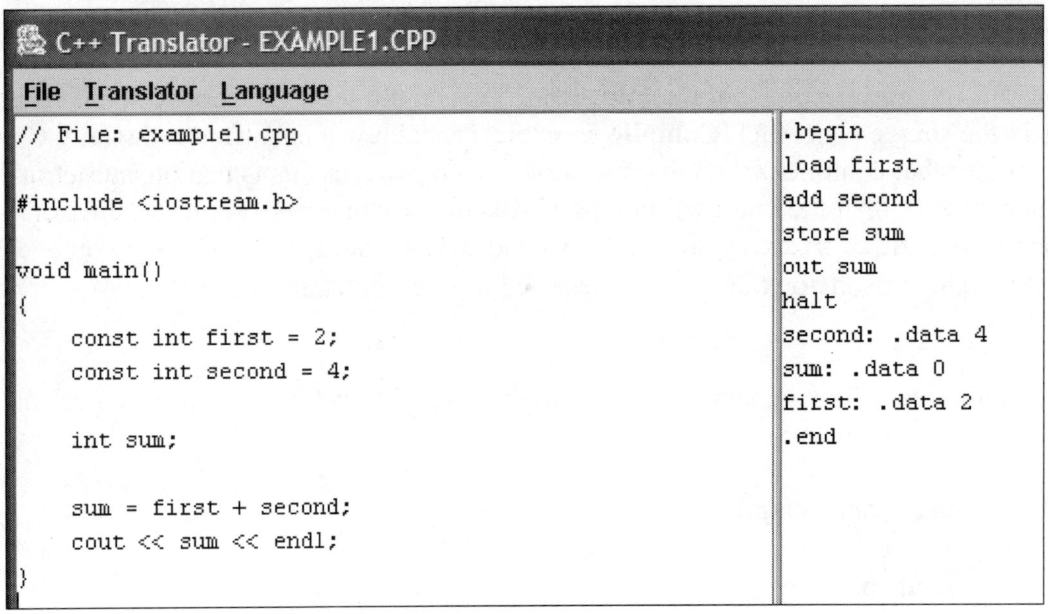

Figure 17.1 The object code of a C++ program

Look at the data declaration part of the assembly language program, and compare that with the data declarations in the C++ program. How many assembly language instructions, on the average, are required to implement a C++ statement? Which C++ statements are the easiest to translate, and which ones seem to be the most difficult?

Exercise 17.8. Translating a C++ loop

Edit the program so that it displays all of the numbers between the first number and the second number (convert the constant definition of **first** to a variable and use it to control the loop). Compile the program and view the object code. You should see an equivalent loop in assembly language.

Exercise 17.9. Code optimization

Examine the translation of the C++ assignment statement **first = first + 1** in the assembly language program. How many instructions does this simple C++ statement require? Explain how the compiler could have translated this C++ assignment statement to one assembly language instruction (*Hint*: change the C++ statement to **++first** and recompile). Explain how the translated program would run more efficiently if the compiler as a rule translated such statements this new way.

Exercise 17.10. Symbol table

Pick **View Symbol Table** from the **Translator** menu. Explain the difference between a C++ constant and a C++ variable. Try putting a C++ constant on the left side of an assignment statement in the C++ program, compile the program, and explain the error message. How do you suppose that the compiler uses the symbol table to translate the C++ program to an assembly language program? Explain the differences between a C++ compiler's symbol table and an assembler's symbol table.

Worksheet
Lab Experience 17
Programming Language Translation

Name: _____

Course: _____

Exercise 17.1. Syntax analysis

Exercise 17.2. Static semantic analysis

Exercise 17.3. Object code

Exercise 17.4. Symbol table

Exercise 17.5. Syntax analysis

a. Delete the word **main**, and compile.

b. Delete the first **{**, and compile.

c. Delete the first assignment operator (**=**), and compile.

d. Delete the addition operator (**+**), and compile.

Exercise 17.6. Static semantic analysis

Exercise 17.7. Object code

Exercise 17.9. Code optimization

Exercise 17.10. Symbol table

Lab Experience 18

Turing Machines (A)

Objectives

- Learn to use a Turing machine simulator that allows you to enter state and transition specifications for a Turing machine and then test the machine with various inputs
- Use a Turing machine simulator to test some of the examples from the textbook
- Make minor modifications to the machines and test the results
- Prepare for working with your own solutions to new problems in the next laboratory session

Background

To get into the Turing machine simulator, click on the **Turing Machine** button of the main button menu of the lab software package. You should now have a window like that shown in Figure 18.1. Briefly, what you see is a window divided into five panes. The **Command** pane contains a set of buttons that you will use to control the simulation once the states, instructions, and tape input have been entered into the simulator. The **Tape** pane is a vertical representation of the tape, with up corresponding to left in the text and down corresponding to right. The darkened cell indicates the current location of the tape head. Skipping to the fourth pane, the **States** pane will contain a list of states that have been defined for the machine. A darkened state will indicate the current state of the machine. The third pane, the **Instructions** pane, will contain the instructions that have been defined for this present state. Recall that an instruction consists of five components: the current state, the input character being read by the tape head, the output character to be written on the tape, the next state to move to, and the direction to move the tape head. If it is the case that there is an instruction for the present state and current tape cell, this instruction will be darkened. Thus, at any time, the Tape pane should represent the current status of the tape and the location of the tape head, the States pane should contain the states with the present state darkened, and the Instructions pane should contain the instructions for the present state with the instruction that applies to the current situation darkened. The **Description** pane contains a description of the current state. It is important to have a clear statement of the situation modeled by a given state. This will be useful to you in finding the source of errors in your machines—the state description doesn't match the current situation—and will make it possible for others (in particular your instructor) to understand what you had in mind when you designed the machine. Finally, there are three important menus at the top of the screen. The **Tape** menu contains options for manipulating the tape, the **Instruction** menu options control the entry and management of instructions, and the **State** menu does the same for the states. We'll cover the details of these as we work on the exercises.

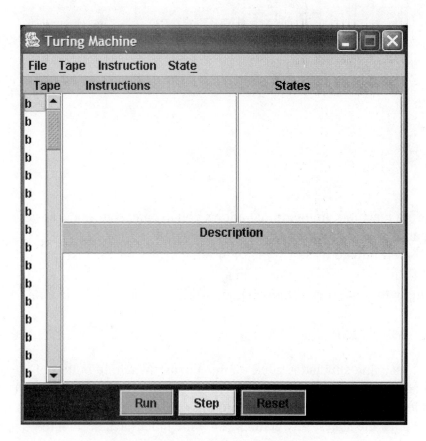

Figure 18.1 The Turing machine simulator

Exercise 18.1. Parity checker

In this exercise, you will work with the parity checker Turing machine that was covered in the text. Recall that this machine adds a 1 to the end of the input string if the string contains an even number of 1's and adds a 0 to the end if the string contains an odd number of 1's. In order to ease into the use of the simulator, you will load in a solution of this problem that we provide for you. You will experiment with the machine with different input strings, and then you will make some changes to the machine and test those. So, to get started, open the **example.sta** file from the **File** menu. After the states are loaded into the simulator, the screen should appear as in Figure 18.2. Notice that there are three states. State 1 is now the current state, and it represents the situation in which we have processed an even number of 1's in the input string. There are three instructions having state 1 as the current state, and the one darkened applies to present state 1 with the tape head being on a blank cell. The darkened instruction "1b13R" in Figure 18.2 applies if we are in state 1 and the current tape symbol is a blank. The third part of an instruction is the symbol to be written in the current tape cell. So, for the darkened instruction, the blank is to be replaced with a 1. The fourth component indicates the next state we move into; here we go to state 3. The final component indicates the direction to move the tape head. So, in words, the instruction "1b13R" says that if we are in state 1, with current symbol blank (b), then we should replace the blank with a 1, move to state 3, and move the tape head to the right. We should also mention that only a portion of the tape is shown at any one time. The simulator proceeds as if there is an indefinite number of cells to the left (up) and to the right (down). When necessary, the pane should scroll to show the appropriate cells. To see the instructions and descriptions for the other two states, simply click on the state in the **States** pane. Go ahead and do this now.

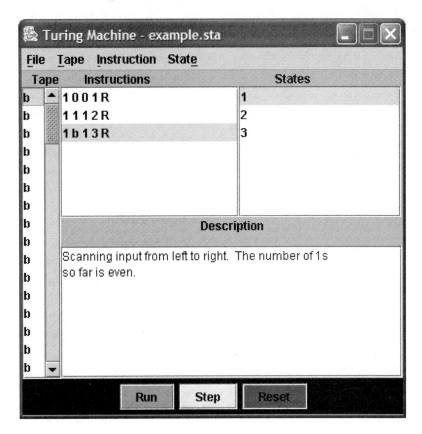

Figure 18.2 Parity checker states loaded

Now to get some initial data on the tape, select the **Open** option from the **Tape** menu. Using the dialog box that appears, find the **Example.tap** file in the **Examples** folder and open it. The machine should now appear as in Figure 18.3. Here we see that the string 110100101 has been loaded onto the tape, the tape head is on the first 1, we are currently in state 1, and the instruction that applies, 1112R, would leave a 1 in this cell, would change to state 2, and would move the tape head to the right (down). Try executing this instruction by clicking on the **Step** button. This button is used to make the simulator execute a single instruction from the present situation. The machine should now appear as in Figure 18.4.

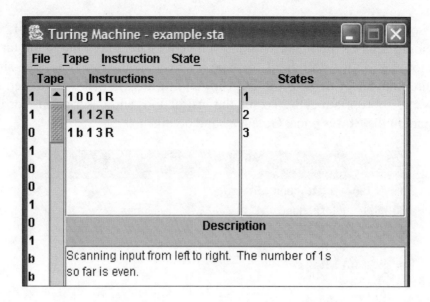

Figure 18.3 Parity checker tape loaded

Notice that we have moved into state 2 and that the tape head has moved to the second 1 in the string. Now continue to follow the execution of the parity checker by clicking the **Step** button three more times and observe the progress each time. For each of these steps, explain the details of what has happened (Worksheet). When you are clear as to how this is working, click on the **Run** button to let the machine run on its own until it finishes its task. A message will now appear informing you that the simulator has halted. Click on the **OK** button to see the final result after the parity bit has been added to the end of the string. Notice that a 0 has been added to the end of the string because the original string contained an odd number of 1's.

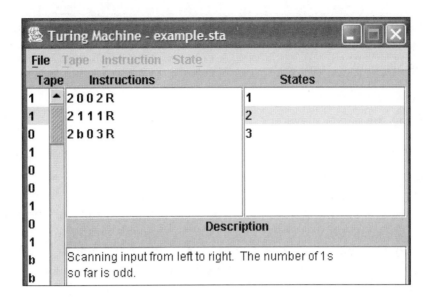

Figure 18.4 Parity checker after first step

The authors' first attempt at solving the parity check problem contained an error. The machine did fine in terms of putting the correct parity bit at the end of the input string. However, it did not know when to stop and kept moving the head to the right over the blanks. By the way, the simulator will continue to add blank cells to either end as the head moves past the end of the visible cells. So, we had a runaway Turing machine on our hands. In case you get tired of watching a run, click on the **Step** button. Don't forget to reset the current state to the start state, which is always state 1.

Exercise 18.2. Parity checker with other input tapes

Now that you have seen the machine operate on this one input string, you should try it out on some other inputs. Select the **Reset** button before editing the tape. The easiest way to manufacture a new input string (without loading it from an existing tape file) is to use the **Initialize** option under the **Tape** menu. This option will allow you to type in a string of symbols that will be loaded into the tape cells. Other options under the **Tape** menu and its nested **Symbol** menu are the following:

- **New** puts blanks (b's) in all of the tape cells.
- **Save as** allows you to save a sample tape string in a tape file for future use.
- **Add** adds a symbol at the left end of the tape string.
- **Delete** removes the current symbol and shifts the tape head to the right.
- **Change** allows you to change the symbol in the selected cell.

Use the **Initialize** option now to enter the string 11111. Test the parity checker by running it on this string and the following strings: 000000, 101010101, and 1. For each of these, give the string that results after the simulator has added the parity bit (Worksheet).

Exercise 18.3. Modifying the parity checker

One important method for solving complex problems is to break the given problem into a series of manageable subproblems. If we can solve the subproblems, then a solution of the main problem can be obtained by letting the output of one subproblem become the input to the next subproblem. In the context of Turing machines, we would want the output tape from one machine to be the input to the next machine. Since we have adopted the convention that the tape head is originally on the first non-blank cell, we would want to be sure that when a machine completes its task, it puts the tape head back on the first non-blank cell. So, let's make the necessary changes to the parity checker so that the tape head is in the proper position when the machine halts.

What changes are necessary? First, once the parity bit is added, we move the head to the left until we come to a blank cell (perhaps out of sight at the top of the Tape pane, originally). Then, we move the head one cell to the right. This can all take place in state 3. However, when the head is moved to the right in the end, we need to change to a new halting state. Otherwise, the new instructions of state 3 would cause the head to move back to the left. Notice that the description for state 3 is no longer accurate since the task is not finished until the head is properly placed. Now select the **Reset** button and make the following required changes to the machine:

1. In the States pane, select state 3. Delete the description for state 3. Enter a new description for state 3, something like "Parity bit added, moving head left to first non-blank cell."

2. Add a new state, state 4, by selecting the **Add** option under the **State** menu. Enter a description, something like "Task completed, tape head back in original position."

3. Change the two instructions that actually add the parity bit so that they move the tape head to the left rather than to the right. To do this, you must first delete the instruction and then add a new instruction. First, select state 1 in the States pane. Then select the instruction (1,b,1,3,R) in the Instructions pane. Choose the **Delete** option under the **Instruction** menu. Now select the **Add** option under this menu. You will be presented with menus for the input symbol (choose b), the output symbol (choose 1), the next state (enter 3), and the tape action (choose L). Now select state 2 and change the instruction (2,b,0,3,R) to (2,b,0,3,L).

4. Add instructions for state 3 that will keep moving the head to the left as long as the input cell is 0 or 1. Select state 3 and add the instructions (3,0,0,3,L) and (3,1,1,3,L).

5.   Finally, add an instruction to move the head back to the right and go into state 4 once the tape head encounters a blank cell in state 3. Select state 3 and add a new instruction (3,b,b,4,R).

Test the altered machine on several input tapes. Notice that each time the machine halts now, the tape head is in position for another run; so try putting the state back to state 1 and clicking on the **Run** button. Try this a few times. What always happens to the parity bit after the first run and why? Answer on the Worksheet.

Exercise 18.4. Producing report for modified parity checker

Assuming that things have gone well so far, you are now ready to produce a report for this exercise. To do this, select the **Save Report** option from the **File** menu. First, you will be prompted for your name. Next, you will be prompted for your course and section number. Enter the appropriate information to identify your lab section as requested by your instructor. When you are prompted for the machine description, give a brief description, something like "Adds a parity bit to the end of a string of 0's and 1's and puts the tape head in the original position." The report will include this information along with a listing of the states together with the state descriptions and instructions. At the end of this process, the report will be sent to a file and you can turn it in electronically or print it from a word processor.

Exercise 18.5. Unary adder

Recall that the unary representation of a non-negative integer consists of a string of 1's with one more 1 than the numerical value of the integer. In this exercise, you will enter and test the Turing machine presented in the text to add two unary numbers. So, starting with a clear machine, add the following states and descriptions: State 1 (Erase the leftmost 1), State 2 (Erase the second 1), State 3 (Scan from left to right and replace the blank separating the two numbers with a 1), and State 4 (Task completed—tape contains the sum of the two input numbers). Next, select State 1 and add the instruction (1,1,b,2,R), select State 2 and add the instruction (2,1,b,3,R), then select State 3 and add the instructions (3,1,1,3,R) and (3,b,1,4,R). Now test the adder with several addition problems. On the Worksheet, give the string that is produced when the original tape contains the string 1111b11111.

Worksheet
Lab Experience 18
Turing Machines (A)

Name: _____

Course: _____

Exercise 18.1. Parity checker

Explain in detail what actions take place when the second step is executed:

Explain in detail what actions take place when the third step is executed:

Explain in detail what actions take place when the fourth step is executed:

Exercise 18.2. Parity checker with other input tapes

Resulting string after parity bit is added to 11111:

Resulting string after parity bit is added to 000000:

Resulting string after parity bit is added to 101010101:

Resulting string after parity bit is added to 1:

Exercise 18.3. Modifying the parity checker

What happens when we run the modified parity checker on its own output?

Explain why this always happens:

Exercise 18.5. Unary adder

Give the string produced when the adder is given input string 1111b11111:

Lab Experience 19

Turing Machines (B)

Objectives

- Design Turing machine solutions to a number of problems varying from easy to fairly challenging
- Use the Turing machine simulator to test your solutions with a variety of inputs
- Get an idea of how, at least theoretically, the simple Turing machine model can solve the same kinds of problems that computers can solve

Background

Although the simulator is designed to allow easy modifications to a machine, it is still much easier to give considerable thought to your solution before entering it into the simulator. It pays to work out descriptions for the states beforehand—if you don't have a clear idea of the role of a state, then there is a good chance that there will be a problem with your solution. Try not to use more states than necessary. One way to know that you need a new state is if you find that you are giving conflicting instructions for the state; i.e., if you are wanting the machine to do two different things from the present state with the same current tape symbol. For example, if you want the machine to replace a 1 with a 0 in some situations, but leave the 1 alone in other situations, these two cases must be modeled by different states. Also, be sure to test your solution with several different input tapes. The fact that the machine works for one input does not mean that it will work for all inputs. It is a good idea to try some rather extreme cases, since these are often the cases that cause trouble. For example, if the input is required to be a string of 1's (with at least one 1), then be sure to see what happens if there is just a single 1.

Exercise 19.1. Tape eraser

Design, enter into the simulator, test, and produce a report for a Turing machine which assumes the tape head is on the first of a string of non-blank characters. The machine should erase all of these characters until it encounters a blank. Draw a state-transition diagram for the machine on the Worksheet.

Exercise 19.2. Increase unary number by 2

Design, enter into the simulator, test, and produce a report for a Turing machine which assumes the tape head is on the first of a string of 1's. The machine should add two more 1's to the right side of this string of 1's. Draw a state-transition diagram for the machine on the Worksheet.

Exercise 19.3. Bit sorter

Design, enter into the simulator, test, and produce a report for a Turing machine which assumes the tape head is on the first of a string of 0's and 1's. The output should be the same number of 0's and the same number of 1's, only with the 0's all appearing before the 1's. For example, if the input were 10011011, then the output should be 00011111. For an algorithm to solve this problem, we suggest you try the following approach: Moving from the left, each time you encounter a 1, replace it with a marker, say an x. Then move to the right to see if there is a 0 to the right of the 1 being processed. If there is, replace the 0 with a 1 and then move back to change the x to a 0. Continue this process until either there are no further 1's or else there are no 0's to the right of a 1. Draw a state-transition diagram for the machine on the Worksheet.

Exercise 19.4. Reverse image

Design, enter into the simulator, test, and produce a report for a Turing machine that makes a copy of its input string, only with the bits in reverse order. For example, if the input string is 110101, then the output tape should contain this string, followed by a blank, followed by the reverse string 101011. Draw a state-transition diagram for the machine on the Worksheet.

Exercise 19.5. Unary subtractor

This is a more challenging exercise. Design, enter into the simulator, test, and produce a report for a Turing machine that takes as input two positive integers in unary form, the first of which is larger than the second. The output should be the difference of the two integers, also in unary form. Draw a state-transition diagram for the machine on the Worksheet.

Worksheet
Lab Experience 19
Turing Machines (B)

Name: _____

Course: _____

Exercise 19.1. Tape eraser

State-transition diagram:

Exercise 19.2. Increase unary number by 2

State-transition diagram:

Exercise 19.3. Bit sorter

State-transition diagram:

Exercise 19.4. Reverse image

State-transition diagram:

Exercise 19.5. Unary subtractor

State-transition diagram:

Lab Experience 20

Discrete Event Simulation

Objectives

- Work with the simulator to model the behavior of real-world systems
- Gather data from the simulator to form conjectures about a system's behavior under varying conditions
- Understand the strengths and weaknesses of modeling

Background

There are many processes that can be studied using discrete event simulation, ranging from traffic patterns on busy urban streets to manufacturing assembly lines. One of the most popular uses is to study the characteristics of businesses such as supermarkets, banks, and fast food restaurants in which customers enter the store and wait in line for service from a cashier or teller. Managers of these businesses seek answers to such important questions as "How many cashiers are needed to adequately serve my customers?" and "How long will the waiting lines become during the busiest part of the day?" By building a simulation and testing a range of different configurations, a model can provide answers to these and other similar questions.

A discrete event simulation model allows users to study the behavior of real-world systems, especially when it is impractical or dangerous to experiment with the systems directly. This laboratory experience allows you to explore the features and capabilities of discrete event simulation by modeling the behavior of a McBurgers take-out restaurant similar to the one described in Chapter 12. The main difference between the textbook's model and the one used in this lab experience that in the lab's model there is a separate waiting line for each cashier. The system that we are modeling is shown in Figure 20.1.

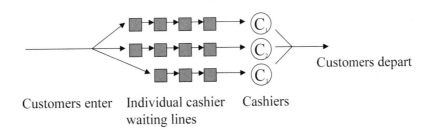

Figure 20.1 The model of a checkout for a take-out restaurant

Our restaurant model cannot be based on a single "magic formula" into which inputs are plugged and answers pop out. If it could, then a simple calculator or spreadsheet would suffice to answer our questions. The reason is that one of the characteristics of these types of businesses is the existence of randomness and variability, what was termed a *stochastic component* in the text. For example, several customers might show up at practically the same instant, while later in the day no one arrives for long stretches of time. Similarly, one customer might order dozens of items while the next one has a cup of coffee. A discrete event simulation model reflects this variability by mimicking the actual real-world process. That is, it uses random numbers to simulate the variability of both customer arrivals and service times.

The model simulates the flow of time by iterating through the program for a specified number of minutes. Each pass through the main loop reflects a single minute of simulated time in the system. On each pass the following three things will occur:

- Zero, one, or more new customers will arrive and go to the end of a cashiers waiting line.
- Each cashier will provide a minute of service time to its current customer, if there is one. If this cashier does not have a customer, then it will be idle.
- If any current customers are completely served during this time unit, they leave their respective cashier lines and the next customer in line becomes the current one.

During this simulation, the program is keeping track of a number of useful statistics, such as the idle and busy time of each cashier, the number of customers served by each cashier, the total waiting time and service time of the customers for each cashier, and so forth. These statistics are displayed at the end of the process.

A user must provide the following four inputs to this discrete event simulation model:

1. The total simulation time as measured in minutes (an integer)
2. The number of cashiers (an integer)
3. The average number of minutes of service time required by each customer (an integer)
4. The probability that a new customer will arrive during the next minute (a real number)

The following table shows the range of legitimate values for each of these four inputs:

Inputs	Range of Legal Values
Total simulation time in minutes	$0 < total <= 1000$
Number of cashiers	$0 < number <= 100$
Average minutes of service time per customer	$0 < service <= total$
Probability of a new customer arrival in the next minute	$0.0 < probability <= 1.0$

The program outputs the following four statistics for each cashier:

- The total number of customers served by this cashier during the simulation
- The number of customers left in this cashier's line when execution ended
- The average time the customer spent in the restaurant, including waiting and service time
- The percentage of time that this cashier was idle

Exercise 20.1. Running the simulation

Select the discrete event simulator. Enter the following four inputs:

> *total* = 60 minutes running time
> *service* = 4 minutes average service time per customer (average cashier speed)
> *probability* = 0.5 probability of arrival
> *number* = 1 cashier

Select the lab software's **Run** button.

Your results should be similar to those shown in Figure 20.2, although they may not be identical because of the random nature of simulation. Fill in the table on the Worksheet with the results from five separate runs of the model using the same inputs. Then fill in the maximum, minimum, and average results for the five runs along the bottom rows. How far from the average values are the minimum and maximum values in each column of results? Does the variability of these results diminish their usefulness or change the manner in which they should be interpreted?

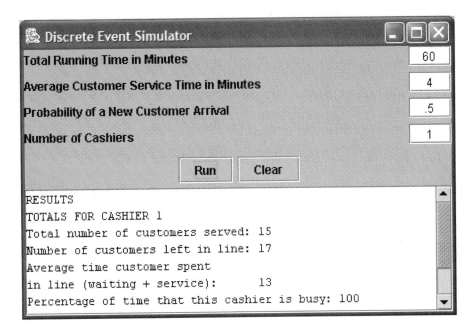

Figure 20.2 The results of a run of the discrete event simulator

Exercise 20.2. Varying the total running time

Run the model using the same values for *number*, *service*, and *probability* used in Exercise 20.1, but with the 5 values of running times given in the table in the Worksheet. Two of these values (20, 30) are smaller than the time used in Exercise 20.1, while three are larger (90, 150, 300). Execute the program three times with each value of the running time and measure the average time that the customer spent in the store. Describe how the variability of the model changes with running time. Discuss what this says about the reliability of the results you get from a discrete event simulation model as a function of how long you run the simulation.

Exercise 20.3. Varying the average customer service time

Run the model using the same values for *total*, *number*, and *probability*, but vary the average customer service time from 1 minute to 8 minutes as shown in the table in the Worksheet. Compare the results with those of Exercise 20.1. Describe the relationship between average customer service time, the total number of customers served, and the number of customers left in line when the model is done running. Explain how this would be an important result if our restaurant wished to add a new menu item that took a long time to prepare.

Exercise 20.4. Varying the probability of a customer arrival

Fill in the table of results on the Worksheet for the same inputs for *total*, *number*, and *service* as in Exercise 20.1 but with the probability of a customer arrival varying from 0.1 to 0.9, modeling a huge increase in the number of customers coming into our restaurant. Compare the results you get with those of Exercise 20.1. Is there a point at which a single cashier can process all of the customers that arrive? Describe in words what is happening to the quality of customer service as the number of customers entering the restaurant increases. What would probably happen in real life?

Exercise 20.5. Varying the number of cashiers

Fill in the table of results on the Worksheet for the same inputs for *total*, *service*, and *probability* as in Exercise 20.1 but with the numbers of cashiers ranging from 1 to 10. Compare the cumulative results with those of Exercise 20.1. Assume that large cashier idle time is just as bad as large customer waiting time and large numbers of customers left in line. What is the optimum number of cashiers? Explain how you determined this value and what you mean by the term "optimum."

Exercise 20.6. Adding variability to the average customer service time

Our simulator asks the user to enter the average number of minutes required to service a customer. However, as it is currently written, the model simply assigns the *same* service time to every customer. Do you think this would produce accurate results? Explain why or why not. In real life, processing times vary randomly around the average. Describe a method of assigning random processing times to customers that would still reflect, on an overall basis, this average time.

Exercise 20.7. Adding variability to the assignment of customers to cashiers

When the user has specified more than one cashier, the simulator assigns customers to cashiers by picking any cashier at random and sending the next customer to the end of that cashier's waiting line. Suggest at least two ways of picking a cashier for a customer that better reflect a real checkout situation and which would increase the accuracy of the model.

Worksheet
Lab Experience 20
Discrete Event Simulation

Name: _____

Course: _____

Exercise 20.1. Running the simulation

Run #	Customers Served	Customers Still in Line	Average Customer Time in Restaurant
1			
2			
3			
4			
5			
Maximum			
Minimum			
Average			

Discussion of Variability:

Exercise 20.2. Varying the total running time

Total Running Time	Average Customer Time in Restaurant (Run 1)	Average Customer Time in Restaurant (Run 2)	Average Customer Time in Restaurant (Run 3)
15			
30			
90			
150			
300			

Discussion of reliability:

Exercise 20.3. Varying the average customer service time

Cashier Speed	Total Customers	Customers Left in Line	Average Wait Time
1			
2			
4			
6			
8			
Averages			

Discussion:

Exercise 20.4. Varying the probability of a customer arrival

Probability of Arrival	Total Customers	Customers Left in Line	Average Wait Time
0.1			
0.2			
0.5			
0.7			
0.9			
Averages			

Discussion:

Exercise 20.5. Varying the number of cashiers

Number of Cashiers	Total Customers	Customers Left in Line	Average Wait Time
1			
2			
3			
4			
5			
10			

Discussion:

Exercise 20.6. Adding variability to the average customer service time

Discussion:

Exercise 20.7. Adding variability to the assignment of customers to cashiers

Suggestion 1:

Suggestion 2:

Lab Experience 21

Database Management

Objectives

- Work with basic SQL Select queries on a single database table
- Use a calculated field with an SQL query
- Use aggregate function to get summary data from database table
- Make SQL queries with related tables of a database

Background

In Section 13.3.2 of the textbook, you were introduced to database management systems and to the Structured Query Language (SQL), which is commonly used to construct queries to extract data from such a database. In this lab session, you will create and test SQL queries with a database similar to the example database in the text.

Since most lab installations are equipped with database systems, we will work with an actual database system rather than a simulation. The examples shown here are based on the Microsoft Access (Office 2000) package. If you are working with a different package, some of the details will be different, but the outcomes should be essentially the same. In this case, your instructor should provide you with modifications to the instructions given here. Access provides several tools for generating queries for the database. However, in this lab, we focus on working directly with SQL.

Included with your lab software is an Access database called **Rugs-For-You.mdb**. You should now open this database by double-clicking on this file or, if you are already running Access, look in the **File** menu and select **Open**. If necessary, click on the **Tables** tab on the left. You should now have a window similar to that of Figure 21.1.

Notice that there are three tables listed—Employees, InsurancePlans, and InsurancePolicies. The Employees table contains the basic name, birth date, and pay information for the employees along with an identification number serving as a primary key. The InsurancePlans table contains information on each type of insurance option provided through the company. The primary key is a plan type. The InsurancePolicies table contains information on the individual policies held by the employees. Along with the date the policy was issued, there are two foreign keys: the employee's identification number and the plan type.

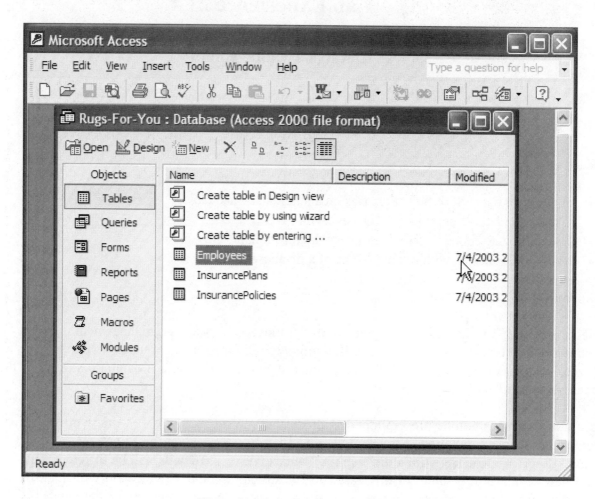

Figure 21.1 Rugs-For-You Database

Exercise 21.1. Relationships

Under the **Tools** menu, select **Relationships**. You should see a figure similar to Figure 21.2. Here the primary keys in the Employees and InsurancePlans tables are shown in bold, as are the two foreign keys in the InsurancePolicies table. The two lines show the primary key for each foreign key. They also show one-to-many relationships, meaning that one employee or one insurance plan can be associated with multiple insurance policies.

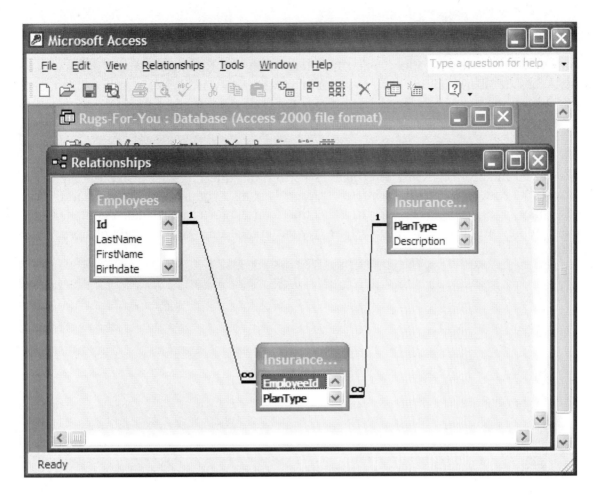

Figure 21.2 Relationships Among the Database Tables

Exercise 21.2. The Employees table—the data

Select the Employees table and click on the **Open** button in the upper-left corner of the Rugs-For-You Database window. You should now see the data currently in the Employees table, as in Figure 21.3. Scan the data to become familiar with the kind of data being stored. In this view you would be able to add, delete, or modify data in the table.

Click on the small + sign beside the employee with ID 149. What do you see? Why do you see it? (*Hint*: think about the relationships between the tables.) Would you expect to see + signs in either of the other two tables? Explain your answers in the Worksheet.

Exercise 21.3. The Employees table—the fields and data types

You should now select **Design View** under the **View** menu, or else click on the Design View button on the Microsoft Access toolbar. In either case you should now see the various fields of the table together with their data types. Fill in the table showing the data types for each field. Click on LastName to see the number of characters (field size) allowed for the last name.

In this view you would be able to add, delete, or modify fields for the table. Notice that the first and last names are stored in separate fields. This enables us to order query results or reports alphabetically by last name and to choose to present names in either order. It is also common practice to store birth dates rather than ages, since ages change once a year and thus cause unnecessary data maintenance. Ages can be computed from the birth dates when needed. Somewhat in the same spirit, we do not store the actual pay, but compute it from the pay rate and the hours worked.

ID	LastName	FirstName	Birthdate	PayRate	HoursWorked
220	Adams	Kenneth	9/18/1973	$20.25	210
193	Doolittle	Iwill	4/21/1982	$6.00	15
165	Honou	Morris	6/9/1988	$6.70	53
171	Kay	John	11/17/1954	$17.80	245
116	Kay	Janet	3/29/1956	$16.60	94
233	Littlehale	Mark	12/12/1969	$21.25	215
291	Miller	John	8/15/1978	$17.80	180
115	Palazzalo	Maria	2/14/1980	$11.75	144
123	Perreira	Francine	8/15/1987	$8.50	185
113	Sauer	Robert	11/22/1971	$19.40	221
149	Takasano	Frederick	5/23/1966	$12.35	250
153	Tziros	Christina	12/23/1982	$19.85	215
132	Wilson	Mary	10/16/1979	$14.40	190
				$0.00	0

Record: 1 of 13

Employee's identification number

Figure 21.3 The Employees table

Next, close the Employees table and click the **Queries** tab on the left. For each of the queries you create in this lab, you will work with the SQL View in Access. To get to that view, double-click on the **Create query in Design View** option, close the **Show Table** window, and then select **SQL View** from the **View** menu.

Exercise 21.4. First query—selecting columns from table

In the Query View window, edit the SELECT statement shown to read:

> SELECT ID, FirstName, LastName, PayRate, HoursWorked
> FROM Employees;

Recall that the SELECT clause specifies the columns that we want from the table(s), and the FROM clause specifies the table(s) to be used. Now select the **Run** option from the **Query** menu. Describe the results.

Exercise 21.5. A computed column

SQL provides some limited capabilities to compute new values from data contained in the fields of the table rows. To see an example of this, go back to SQL View and edit the statement to read:

> SELECT ID, LastName, PayRate, HoursWorked, PayRate*HoursWorked As Pay
> FROM Employees;

Here we have asked that the query contain a column, named Pay, which is computed by multiplying together the values in the PayRate and HoursWorked fields. Test the statement by running the query.

Write an SQL query to compute overtime pay where all hours worked are paid at time-and-a-half.

Run your query; what is the overtime pay for Wilson?

Exercise 21.6. Computing the employees' ages

To compute the ages of an employee, we would subtract the birth date from the current date. Various implementations of SQL provide slightly different methods for obtaining the current date. With Access, this is given by the Date function. Now go back into SQL View and change the SQL statement to:

> SELECT LastName,BirthDate, Date() - BirthDate As Age
> FROM Employees;

and then run the query. As you see, there is a problem with this query—the result is giving the number of days the employee has been alive rather than the number of years. To correct this, change the computation to be

> (Date() – BirthDate)/365

and run again. We're getting closer, but we probably prefer to have the age expressed as an integer. In Access we can get the desired result by editing the computation to

$$Int((Date() - BirthDate)/365$$

Make this change and test again. You should get results as shown in Figure 21.4.

LastName	Birthdate	Age
Sauer	11/22/1971	31
Palazzalo	2/14/1980	23
Kay	3/29/1956	47
Perreira	8/15/1987	15
Wilson	10/16/1979	23
Takasano	5/23/1966	37
Tziros	12/23/1982	20
Honou	6/9/1988	15
Kay	11/17/1954	48
Doolittle	4/21/1982	21
Adams	9/18/1973	29
Littlehale	12/12/1969	33
Miller	8/15/1978	24

Figure 21.4 Computed Age column

Exercise 21.7. Choosing rows from the table

Recall that the WHERE clause in an SQL statement specifies conditions that must be met in order for a row to appear in the result of the query. Now return to SQL View and modify the previous query to give information only for the employee with last name Kay. What are the results when you run the query now?

Exercise 21.8. A query with two tables

If you have not done so, you should scan the fields and data of the other two tables now. The information here is separated into two tables to avoid considerable redundancy. For example, the description of a plan type should not appear with every policy issued for that type since this would waste a lot of storage space, and, more importantly, would create a nightmare in terms of maintaining the data. For example, a slight change in the description of a plan type would require making the change in all policy records for that plan type. You will see how the relational model allows us to bring together related data from different tables.

Suppose we want a query to show the cost of the plan along with the policy information. The key here is that the PlanType field for the two tables "links" the policy from the InsurancePolicies table with the insurance plan in the InsurancePlans table. To see how this works, back in the query SQL View, enter the statement:

> SELECT EmployeeID, InsurancePolicies.PlanType, DateIssued, MonthlyCost
> FROM InsurancePolicies, InsurancePlans
> WHERE InsurancePolicies.PlanType = InsurancePlans.PlanType;

and run the query. Note that we must qualify the field name with the table name where both tables have a field with the given name. In this example, the WHERE clause is being used to "join" the two tables, combining rows from the two tables that agree in the PlanType fields. How are the results of the query ordered?

Exercise 21.9. Ordering the rows of a query result

Recall that the ORDER BY clause of an SQL query allows us to have the result sorted by the values of one or more fields. For the query of Exercise 21.8, suppose we would like to have the results ordered by the Employee ID. What should be added to the SQL query after the WHERE clause? Add this, and run the query again.

Exercise 21.10. Combining the three tables

Suppose now that we would like the employees' names to appear rather than the identification numbers. The names are found only in the Employees table. The link we have now is that the EmployeeID field in the InsurancePolicies table corresponds to the ID field in the Employees table. In SQL View, change the statement to:

> SELECT FirstName, LastName, InsurancePolicies.PlanType, DateIssued, MonthlyCost
> FROM Employees, InsurancePolicies, InsurancePlans
> WHERE
>   InsurancePolicies.PlanType = InsurancePlans.PlanType AND ID = EmployeeID
> ORDER BY LastName, FirstName;

The result should be as shown in Figure 21.5.

Exercise 21.11. Using GROUP BY and an aggregate function

As a final example to show some of the features of SQL, suppose that we wish to group all of the policies for an individual employee and show the total insurance cost for all of the employee's policies. The GROUP BY clause is used to "squash" related rows of the query result into a single row. Of course, the rows being combined this way must agree in all fields. SQL provides functions, called **aggregate functions**, which can be applied to these grouped rows to give summary data of certain kinds. One such function is the Sum function, which gives a total for a numeric field for the various groups. In SQL View, change the statement to:

SELECT FirstName, LastName, Sum(MonthlyCost) As Cost
FROM Employees, InsurancePolicies, InsurancePlans
WHERE
    InsurancePolicies.PlanType = InsurancePlans.PlanType AND ID = EmployeeID
GROUP BY LastName, FirstName
ORDER BY LastName, FirstName;

Run this query and write the first three rows of the result.

FirstName	LastName	PlanType	DateIssued	MonthlyCost
Kenneth	Adams	B3	7/23/1999	$400.00
John	Kay	C1	6/21/1982	$10.00
John	Kay	B2	10/18/1974	$250.00
Mark	Littlehale	B1	1/14/1992	$150.00
Mark	Littlehale	A2	1/14/1992	$20.00
Mark	Littlehale	A1	1/14/1992	$50.00
John	Miller	B1	4/15/2001	$150.00
Robert	Sauer	B3	3/17/1996	$400.00
Robert	Sauer	C2	3/17/1996	$30.00
Frederick	Takasano	C2	12/16/1999	$30.00
Frederick	Takasano	B2	8/16/1990	$250.00
Frederick	Takasano	A1	5/23/1995	$50.00
Christina	Tziros	C1	8/11/2003	$10.00
Christina	Tziros	C2	8/11/2003	$30.00
Christina	Tziros	B3	5/12/2003	$400.00
Mary	Wilson	B1	10/18/2001	$150.00

Query1 : Select Query

Figure 21.5 The three-table query

Worksheet
Lab Experience 21
Database Management

Name: _____

Course: _____

Exercise 21.2. The Employees table—the data

The + sign:

Exercise 21.3. The Employees table—the fields and data types

Field Name	Data Type
Id	
LastName	
FirstName	
Birthdate	
PayRate	
HoursWorked	

   Field size for LastName:

Exercise 21.4. First query—selecting columns from table

Describe query results:

Exercise 21.5. A computed column

   SQL query for overtime:

Overtime pay for Wilson:

Exercise 21.7. Choosing rows from the table

Modified SQL query:

Query results:

Exercixe 21.8. A query with two tables

How are the results of the query ordered?

Exercise 21.9. Ordering the rows of a query result

What should be added to the SQL query?

Exercise 21.11. Using GROUP BY and an aggregate function

First three rows of the result of running the query:

Lab Experience 22

Data Encryption

Objectives

- Understand the purpose of data encryption
- Understand a simple algorithm for data encryption

Background

Data encryption plays a major role in computer applications, ranging from simple logins for system accounts to secure transmission of information over a network. The purpose of data encryption is to transform data into a secure form so they can be accessed only by those who have authorization to do so. In this lab, we assume that the datum is a string of characters. This datum is input to the encryption algorithm, which outputs another string in encrypted or encoded form. The encoded string can in turn be input to a decryption algorithm to recover the original string.

The particular encryption and decryption algorithms used in this lab are fairly simple. They employ a data structure called an encryption matrix. The encryption matrix is a two-dimensional grid of characters. The grid has 8 rows and 12 columns. Thus, there are just enough cells in this grid to hold the 95 printable characters on the keyboard, plus the bell character. The characters are inserted into the encryption matrix in random order, as shown in Figure 22.1.

!	□	S	r	B	0	_	L	V	P	\	Z
.	g	I	K	v	5	w	q	N	'	{	3
0	s	)	;	U	b	H	n	J	&	8	:
<		C	*	G	a	(	o	h	m	p	4
e	c	y	k	Q	9	X	}	t	E	W	T
-	>	6	j	1	^	d	F	D	f	x	i
[	|	,	A	z	2	/	%	?	1	]	+
M	Y	u	R	7	`	#	@	$	~	"	=

Figure 22.1 An encryption matrix

Informally, the encryption algorithm uses the encryption matrix as follows:

1. Scan through the input string from left to right, two characters at a time.
2. Locate the positions of a given pair of characters in the encryption matrix.
3. If these positions are in the same row or the same column, then swap the characters in the input string to form an encoded pair of characters.
4. Otherwise, locate the characters at the remaining corners of the rectangle formed by these positions, and use these characters to form an encoded pair of characters.
5. Concatenate all of the encoded pairs of characters to form the output string.
6. If the length of the input string is odd, append the last character of the original input string to the output string.

The decryption algorithm simply uses the encryption algorithm with an encoded string as input to produce the original string.

Exercise 22.1. Running the encryption simulator

Launch the encryption simulator by clicking the lab software's **Encryption Simulator** button. Enter the string "Hello there!" in the **Original String** field and click the **Encrypt** button. The encrypted string should appear in the **Encrypted String** field. Figure 22.2 shows a sample run.

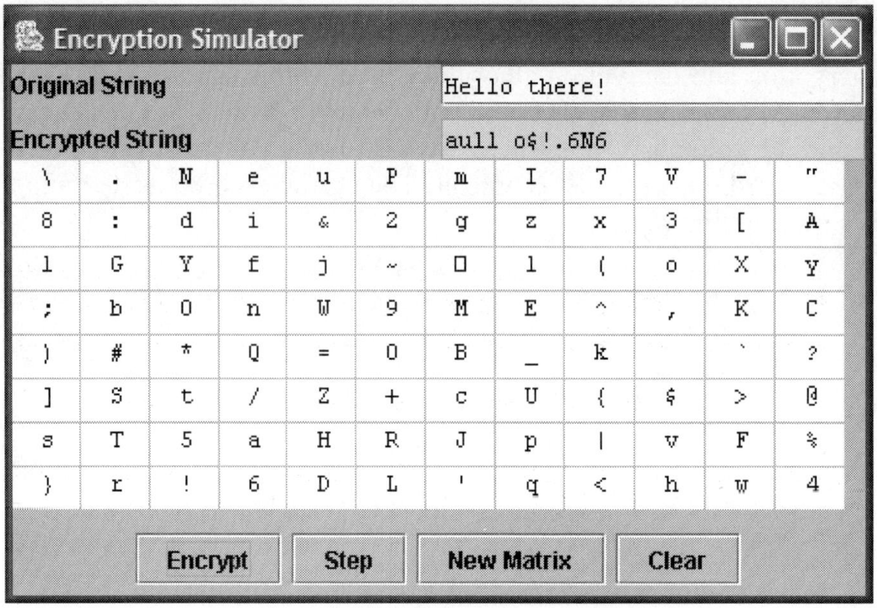

Figure 22.2 A run of the encryption simulator

Note that your encrypted string will likely be different from the one in this screen shot, because your matrix will likely be different. Write down the encrypted string you get in the Worksheet.

Exercise 22.2. Choosing a different encryption matrix

Now click the **New Matrix** button. A new randomly generated encryption matrix should appear. Click **Encrypt** again to verify that a new matrix generates a different encoding. Click **Clear** to clear the data fields. Now try encrypting your full name and then a password you have used when working with a computer.

Exercise 22.3. Stepping through the process

Click **Clear** to clear the data fields and enter the string "Hello again." Instead of clicking **Encrypt**, repeatedly click the **Step** button and observe the changes in the encryption matrix (see Figure 22.3).

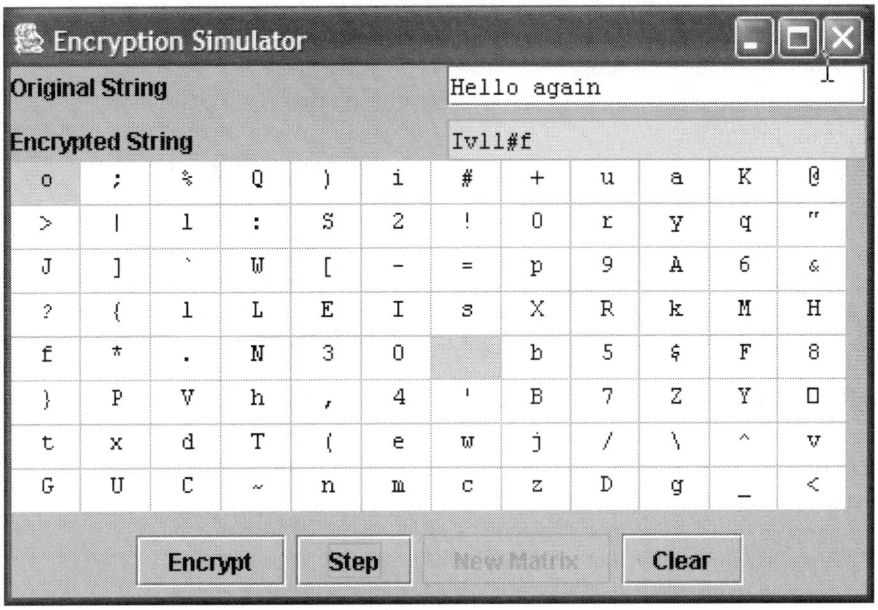

Figure 22.3 Stepping through the encryption process

As you step through the encryption process, each pair of encoded characters (the ones shaded in the matrix) is added to the encrypted string. Visually locate the rectangle formed by each pair of original characters and their encodings. Describe what happens when a pair of characters falls in the same row or column in the matrix. Describe what happens when the last character (the odd one) is processed.

Exercise 22.4. Refining the algorithm

Rewrite Step 4 of the encryption algorithm to specify the order in which the characters found at the remaining corners of the rectangle are used.

Exercise 22.5. Decryption

Enter a short phrase and encrypt it. Now copy the encrypted string and click the **Clear** button. Enter the encrypted string as the original string and click the **Encrypt** button. What is the result?

Repeat this experiment, but this time select a new matrix before you click the **Encrypt** button. What is the result?

Exercise 22.6. Explanation

Explain why this encryption algorithm is its own inverse, that is, why running the algorithm on encrypted data returns the original data.

Exercise 22.7. Repeating characters

Click **Clear** to clear the data fields. Then enter the string "AABBCC" and click **Encrypt**. Describe what is peculiar about the encoded string and explain why this happens.

Exercise 22.8. An improvement

Do you think that a problem is caused when a string having repeating characters or an odd number of characters is encrypted with this method? How would you change the algorithm to solve this problem?

Worksheet
Lab Experience 22
Data Encryption

Name: _____

Course: _____

Exercise 22.1. Running the encryption simulator

Original string _____

Encrypted string _____

Exercise 22.3. Stepping through the process

A pair of characters falls in the same row or column in the matrix:

The last character (the odd one) is processed:

Exercise 22.4. Refining the algorithm

Exercise 22.5. Decryption

Result of encrypting the encrypted data:

Result of encrypting the encrypted data with a new matrix:

Exercise 22.6. Explanation

Exercise 22.7. Repeating characters

Exercise 22.8. An improvement

Lab Experience 23

Neural Networks

Objectives

- Gain experience working with a neural network for character recognition
- Work with the phases of telling the network the characters to recognize, providing test data, and testing the accuracy of the recognition

Background

A neural network consists of a set of input nodes, a set of output nodes, and one or more hidden layers of nodes that connect the input nodes to the output nodes. Input and output nodes can represent patterns, such as characters or images of faces, to be recognized by the network. For example, in the case of characters, pieces of a character in a visual field can map to individual input nodes in the network. To acquire knowledge of this pattern, the user trains the net by giving it the pattern as a desired output node and asking the net to train itself. The net trains itself by placing this pattern on its input nodes and running perhaps several iterations until the connections from input nodes to the output node reach a certain value. After the net has been trained to recognize a given pattern, the user can present it with this pattern or a similar one as a trial input and ask the net to solve for the input pattern. If the input pattern is similar enough to one of the patterns represented in the net's set of output nodes, the net informs the user that it recognizes the input as the pattern represented by that node; otherwise, the net does not recognize the input pattern.

The neural net simulator provides you with the following features:

1. A built-in network
2. The ability to draw new output nodes (patterns to be recognized)
3. The ability to train the net to recognize these patterns
4. The ability to give the net trial patterns as inputs and attempt to solve for them.

Open the neural net lab by clicking **Neural Network** from the main menu. You should see the window shown in Figure 23.1.

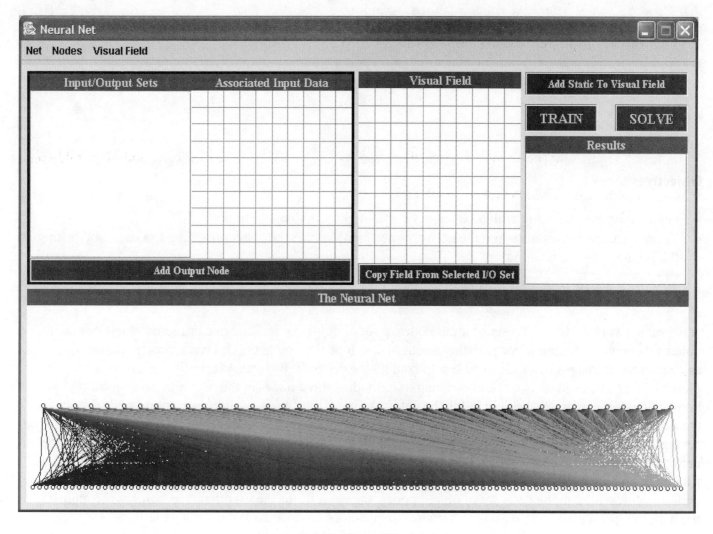

Figure 23.1 The Neural Net window

The neural net window consists of the following panes:

1. **Input/Output Sets** (upper-left pane). Here you can edit patterns to be added as output nodes to the net. You can transfer these patterns to and from files or from the **Visual Field** (see below).
2. **Visual Field** (upper-middle pane). Here you can edit patterns to be presented as trial inputs to the net. You can transfer these patterns to and from files or from the **Input/Output Sets**.
3. **Results** (upper-right pane). The results of training or solving are displayed here.
4. **The Neural Net** (lower pane). Here is a visual representation of the neural net. The input nodes are at the bottom, and the output nodes are at the top.

The three menus allow you to manage the net, the output nodes, and the visual field.

Exercise 23.1. Training the network to recognize the letter A

In this exercise, you will train the network to recognize the letter A. A training session consists of entering the character to be learned and training the net. To get started, perform the following steps:

1. Click the **Add Output Node** button.
2. Enter the letter A in the prompter, click the radio button **Visual Field From File**, and click **OK** (see Figure 23.2).
3. Select the file **Character'A'.vfl** and click **OK**.

Figure 23.2 Adding an output node for the letter A

Then click **Train**. Your application window should look like the one in Figure 23.3.

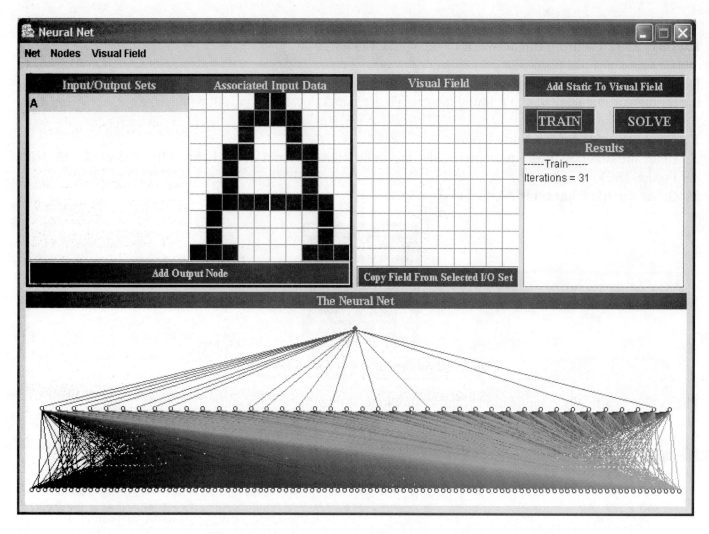

Figure 23.3 Training a neural network for the letter A

Note that the net now has a single output node. Each connection from this node to the net represents a black square in the pattern for the letter A. The net also took 31 iterations to learn this letter. The number of iterations may be different for your training session.

Exercise 23.2. Solving for a test character

Let's test the recognition capability of the network trained in the previous exercise. There three ways to create a sample pattern for input:

1. Click the button **Copy Field From Selected I/O Set**.
2. Open a visual field pattern from a file (**Visual Field** menu).

3. Draw the pattern by hand (clicking the squares in the visual field pane).

Step 1 is the easiest, so do that now. Then click the **Solve** button. Your window should look like the one in Figure 23.4.

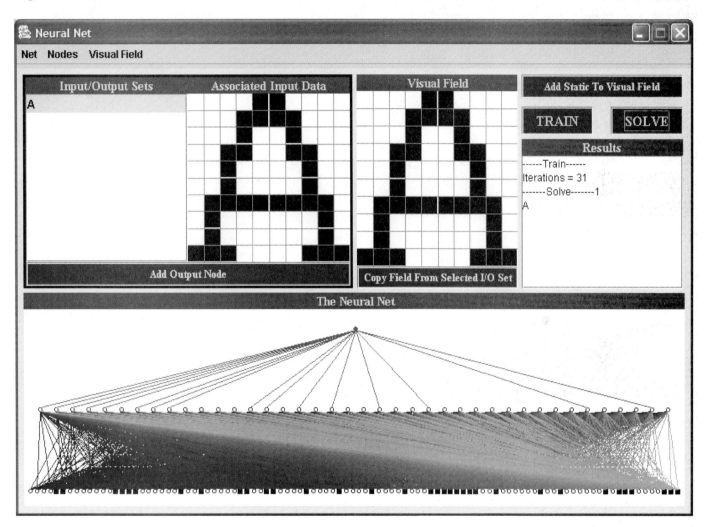

Figure 23.4 Solving for the letter A

The window now has several changes:

1. The input pattern appears in the Visual Field pane.
2. The input nodes corresponding to the black squares in this pattern are highlighted in the net.
3. The results of recognizing the input pattern are displayed in the Results pane.

Exercise 23.3. Editing a test character

Human beings are able to recognize letters and other objects even though they might only be approximations of some ideal types. To test the neural net's recognition capability, we can remove pieces of the letter A and observe the outputs. Remove the top two dots on the bitmap by right-clicking the mouse on them. Then select **Solve**. Now try removing one dot at a time from the next row and solving each time. Describe what the character looks like to you.

Exercise 23.4. Training for more than one character

The real power of a neural network lies in its ability to distinguish several different objects. To see how this is so, let's train a net to recognize the letters A, B, and O. To clear the current network, select **New** from the **Net** menu. You will see a dialog box that allows you to specify the resolution of the visual field, the number of hidden nodes, and the percent of connectivity. Leave the defaults in place and click **Create the Net**. Then, click **Add Output Node** three times to enter the three letters from their respective files. When you click **Train**, the network learns the three characters concurrently. After training, your window should look like the one in Figure 23.5.

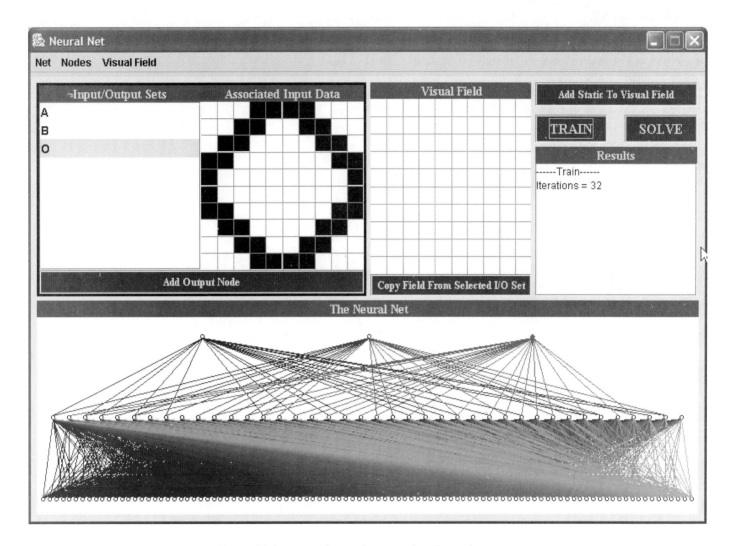

Figure 23.5 A neural net after entering three characters

Try solving for each input letter after placing each letter in the visual field pane. Now delete the top two rows of squares in the visual field's letter A and solve. Explain the results.

Exercise 23.5. How much can the net handle?

Add a character at a time to the I/O set for the net from Exercise 23.4 and train after each one is entered. You might have to click the **Train** button several times before the net is trained for a given character. Then explain the results.

Worksheet
Lab Experience 23
Neural Networks

Name: _____

Course: _____

Exercise 23.2. Solving for a test character

Exercise 23.3. Editing a test character

Exercise 23.4. Training for more than one character

Exercise 23.5. How much can the net handle?